T0356250

PRAISE FOR

Becoming Girlilla

JENNIE'S STORY is a master class in what it means to have your hard work pay off. An inspiring life story (both personal and professional) for any reader, especially women, that will fuel your creative soul and leave you feeling inspired to do anything. That's what Jennie did and continues to do every day: break industry molds and boundaries, be the face and role model for aspiring media junkies alike, and overall, proves to be one badass girl boss. When it comes to media or just being a plain 'ole good person, you want Jennie in your life.

—KRISTIN CHENOWETH
Artist, Performer, Actress, Author, and Philanthropist

BECOMING GIRLILLA will make you cry, laugh, light a blazing fire under your ass to chase your dreams, and most importantly, encourage you to listen to that quiet but powerful inner voice we all have. Jennie writes with a rawness that is so refreshing and warm. *Becoming Girlilla* is "chicken soup for the soul."

—MADDIE FONT
Recording Artist (Maddie & Tae)

THERE'S A FINE LINE between success and failure. That difference is often defined by sheer will and determination. Jennie exemplifies that with articulate reflection and vulnerability. I've known her for years, and I've always been impressed by her knowledge and strength of character. As I read through Jennie's journey, I was moved by her ability to share her pain and childhood trauma while navigating the shark-filled waters of the entertainment business. It's a story filled with hope, success, and failure, with a deep love for this crazy thing called the music business.

—TRACY LAWRENCE
Artist, Entrepreneur, and Philanthropist

UNFLINCHING, UNFILTERED, HONEST, transparent, and inspiring. Jennie's story is one that anyone can relate to no matter what career path they've chosen or what season of life they're in.

From page one you're dropped into the middle of Jennie's life, and with each turn of the page, you're immediately drawn in by her unique sense of humor, brutal honesty, and candor.

Jennie's sometimes unbelievable story is a fun, easy ride that will challenge you to push yourself beyond what you perceive to be your limits, while at the same time, giving you a virtual handbook of things to avoid from lessons that she sometimes had to learn the hard way.

So if you're looking for some motivation, or you need a little (hard) shove to finally go out and make your dreams a reality, this is the perfect guide from someone who has overcome great obstacles and defeated giants with strength, tenacity, and determined resolve. A fantastic read but she does have a filthy mouth!

—JAY DEMARCUS, Recording Artist
(Rascal Flatts) and CEO, Red Street Records

I'VE HAD THE PRIVILEGE of witnessing Jennie's incredible journey from our early days together in the music business. We started our careers around the same time, and while our paths have been different, our friendship solidified so many years ago is unwavering. Her bravery in writing this book, in building a successful digital marketing company from the ground up, and in fighting cancer, combined with her vulnerability, humor, and determination, is a true inspiration. She's not just an example of success for women or young people—she shows that you don't have to compromise your integrity or be ruthless to achieve success.

—CARIANNE MARSHALL
Cochair and COO Warner Chappell Music

Becoming Girlilla is full of hysterical truths, difficult decisions and so much resilience. Jennie Smythe is a trail blazer who started her digital marketing business over fifteen years ago, and this book shares her story and her beautiful heart. This read is sure to bring you laughs and tears. It is full of love, support, hardships, friendships, and a few f-bombs. Jennie assures you that not everything online deserves your energy, and preschool should have prepared you on how to interact on social media. Lesson one: BE NICE!

—SLOANE CAVITT LOGUE, WME

I MET JENNIE when she was an assistant at Elektra Records. I knew her employers well. She was raised by wolves, though much of her job was herding cats—albeit often feral ones. The young woman I met back then took her daily challenges in stride with the grace of someone considerably older.

We became instant friends, and I watched with admiration as she ventured down fresh paths in the early days of digital and became explorer in new terrain that would eventually transform everything. Her confidence never wavered.

Over the years, I watched her build a company, start a family, and battle the Big C. She was there for friends facing similar challenges. She remained strong for everyone, even when those in her circle lost the same battles. I am humbled and inspired by what she has given back to the music community through her work with various nonprofit organizations that facilitate healthcare and awareness.

That said: Get screened early and often, or she will kick your ass.

—**TODD HENSLEY**
COO HITS Magazine, HITSDailyDouble.com

LIFE HAS A WAY of bringing us unexpected mentors, even from the most unlikely places. Jennie's estranged father was one such figure—a man whose advice, given during a poignant moment of his own life, ignited a spark in Jennie that led her to embrace her passions and chart her own path. It was his simple yet profound question—"If you knew your life was half over, what would you do with the rest of it?"—that pushed her to pursue her dream of working in the music industry, a decision that would not only change her life but also inspire countless others.

In *Becoming Girlilla*, Jennie takes us on an incredible journey of resilience, ambition, and reinvention. Despite facing immense challenges, including a breast cancer diagnosis, raising two children, and building her own company from the ground up, Jennie refused to let adversity define her. She continued to lead her business, raise her family, and fight for her dreams. She had angels who helped her through the cancer. Her former boss, Jay Frank, and my wife Phran would be there for her to add support, humor, and words of encouragement when she needed them. Unfortunately, they lost their cancer battles, but Jennie uses what she has learned to help others on similar journeys.

Jennie's story is as much about survival as it is about transformation. It's about turning pain into purpose, learning from the past, and carving out a legacy built on strength, compassion, and innovation. Her father's advice may have been the catalyst, but it was Jennie's courage, creativity, and relentless drive that turned her dreams into reality.

This book is a testament to the power of believing in yourself and embracing the opportunities that come your way, no matter how daunting they may seem. Whether you're battling your own struggles or striving to achieve your dreams, *Becoming Girlilla* will leave you inspired, empowered, and ready to face life head on.

—**JOE GALANTE,** Former Chairman
Sony Music Nashville, Entrepreneur, and Philanthropist

Becoming Girlilla is a raw, authentic look at life for anyone who still dreams, still hopes for magic in life, and needs a little kick in the ass to answer the question, "What would you do if you knew your life was half over?" It's a guidebook for life, with a beautiful mix of humor, lessons on hustle and kindness, resilience, friendship, and loyalty. The underlying theme throughout also addresses and advises on the music business and takes a real look at the harsh reality it offers and the dangers and joys of social media. An addicting, entertaining, and heartfelt read.

—JOJAMIE HAHR, EVP, BMG Nashville

JENNIE HAD A FRONT ROW seat for the digital explosion in music marketing and takes us on a fun ride back to help us all determine our future. Her highly personal story mirrors the evolving media business—where art and commerce collide. This is a highly readable book for all—digital music marketers, entrepreneurs, and especially cancer survivors. Her personal story of finding her path is relatable to many. Her passion for the power of direct-to-consumer engagement AND the responsibility that comes with it is clear. The heart, humor, and inspiration in her story makes this a quick, can't-put-it-down read.

—SARAH TRAHERN
CEO Country Music Association

JENNIE IS ONE of the strongest women I know. In this book, I fell in love with her incredible honesty page after page, as she showed us how that muscle was built. And it started with a powerful question that became her North: "If you knew your life was half over, what would you do?" That question made me think about my own life as I read about Jennie creating and living hers—not only as a wildly successful CEO, but as a wife, mother, friend, cancer survivor, and now, author. Jennie has helped so many people find and use their authentic voices. I'm so glad we can read—and be inspired by—hers.

—LAURA OKMIN, NFL on Fox, GALvanize

BECOMING GIRLILLA is a clever, cool, honest, and totally Jennie Smythe telling of an incredible person's story. Her talent, grit, creativity, and straight-up goodness resound on every page. I had the privilege of caring for Jennie during an unbelievably tough time for any person. Although I didn't know what her life looked like before her diagnosis, I have been blessed to be a part of Jennie's journey since. Honestly, she has made a bigger impact on my journey since. God is good like that. I am so proud for you, Jennie. What an incredible story, incredibly told. Humbled to know you and call you my *Pal*.

—KENT "KYE" HIGDON, MD, FACS

JENNIE REDEFINES her life's purpose and shares a candid look at fifteen years of running Girlilla Marketing. As she navigates her own cancer diagnosis and the trials of motherhood, she learns the true meaning of impact. This book isn't just a reflection on success; it's a call to action. It explores how personal struggles can also lead to a desire for meaningful connections and social engagement. Jennie transforms her self-serving ambitions into a mission to uplift others. Readers will find practical tips to set boundaries, reclaim their time, and discover how small changes can lead to a more fulfilling digital experience.

—JILL FRITZO, Jill Fritzo Public Relations

BECOMING GIRLILLA by Jennie Smythe isn't just a book—it's a master class in surviving and thriving in the entertainment industry and in life with grit, guts, and great lipstick. Jennie takes you on a no-holds-barred journey of straightaway successes and head-bumping, pothole-strewn sidetracks, proving all the while that brilliance and street smarts go hand-in-hand. She's a beast in business, a hands-on mom, a pro with hair and makeup, and unapologetically honest—no sugarcoating, no fluff, no apologies. If you've ever wanted to know what it takes to pioneer the digital frontier while keeping your soul intact, then buckle up, buttercup; this book is as real and wild as the industry itself. It will make you laugh, cry, and maybe even see if you have what it takes to become a Girlilla too.

—TATUM HAUCK ALLSEP
Founder and CEO, Music Health Alliance

JENNIE'S MEMOIR is smart, funny, and inspiring—just like the author herself. As an entrepreneur, I found her journey relatable and learned through her own story things I can apply to my own business. And as a human, her guidance for how to have a more responsible digital presence inspires me to be a better person, both online and in real life. A must-read for anyone in the entertainment business!

—CINDY HUNT, Monarch Publicity

JENNIE'S PERSPECTIVE on digital marketing business is so insanely unique because she's one of the few people who got to have success in the marketing world both pre-social media and post-social media revolution. Her career is literally like no one else's, and it's one that you will gain a world of knowledge from seeing the tiniest glimpse of what she's seen.

—CASSIE PETREY, Cofounder, Crowd Surf

IN THE END, I learned a lot from Jennie. She is the epitome of intelligence, grit, and compassion. Jennie is not afraid to take risks and forge her own path—this book offers an unflinching look at her remarkable journey. My conclusion? I want her in the bunker with me.

—BERNIE CAHILL
Founding Partner, Activist Artists Management

JENNIE'S BOOK READS like a powerful ballad—authentic, heartfelt, and inspiring. Having had the privilege of working with Jennie for many years and calling her a loyal friend, I was reminded through her book of her remarkable ability to inspire, lead, and tackle life's challenges with humor and unstoppable drive. She fearlessly addresses tough topics, reflecting on her career and battle with cancer with vulnerability, perseverance, and humility, while generously sharing the lessons she's learned along the way. This is a must-read for anyone chasing their dreams and seeking an uplifting perspective.

—LIZ NORRIS,
Partner, Activist Artists Management

Becoming Girilla

MY JOURNEY TO UNLEASHING GOOD IN REAL LIFE, ONLINE, AND IN OTHERS

JENNIE SMYTHE

RESOLVE
EDITIONS

Published by Resolve Editions, an imprint of Forefront Books.
Distributed by Simon & Schuster.

Library of Congress Control Number: 2024925859

Print ISBN: 978-1-63763-397-7
E-book ISBN: 978-1-63763-398-4

Cover Design by Mary Susan Oleson, Blu Design Concepts
Interior Design by Mary Susan Oleson, Blu Design Concepts

Printed in the United States of America

"Be Good."

— E.T. the Extra-Terrestrial

CONTENTS

If You Knew Your Life Was Half Over

· 2008 ·

I STEPPED INTO the dark room in the dingy health-care facility in Long Beach, California, and gasped. My father, Pete, who was undergoing care for end-stage pancreatic cancer, had declined dramatically in the three days since I'd last seen him. His shrunken body was huddled under the yellowed sheets draped over his wasting form. His eyes were closed.

Pete was losing interest in life.

Fear vise-gripped my heart. The room smelled of crisp antiseptic that didn't mask the musky blend of perspiration and bodily fluids. The glare off the overhead fluorescent lights felt wrong for dying, but that's what was happening.

For years I had envisioned leaving my father to die alone as payback for all the heartache he put me through, all the times he got drunk and embarrassed me. Our relationship had turned bitter in my teens when he cheated on my mother and my parents divorced. After that, he didn't put much effort into keeping in touch with me and my older sister, Kelley. I started calling him by his first name then.

Despite his poor parenting track record, Pete had tried to be more involved in my life over the last ten years. Now, in my late twenties, I finally had a new adult friendship with Pete. My hopes for a meaningful connection with him weren't high, but for the first time in years, I had them.

Since his cancer diagnosis three months earlier, I'd made multiple cross-country trips from my home in Nashville, Tennessee, to be with him as much as possible while simultaneously juggling my job and home responsibilities. I felt worn down and exhausted. But unlike those earlier days when I'd hoped Pete would die alone, all I wanted now was as much time with him as possible.

Pete must have heard me gasp. He opened his eyes and turned his head toward me. "Hey," he said, his voice raspy from lack of use. He coughed to clear his throat. "If you knew your life was half over, what would you do?"

He caught me off guard. My whole body drew away from the inquiry, as if it could be avoided. "What kind of question is that?"

"A really important one." Pete's eyes were glassy, but he seemed very alert. He asked again, "If you knew your life was half over, what would you do with the rest of it?"

I drew in a breath. I had been dreaming about several goals but hadn't yet shared them with anyone or taken any action.

"Well," I began slowly, "I want to start my own digital marketing agency." I let that hang in the space between us. The idea seemed far-fetched and even audacious, but speaking it aloud sent eagerness and optimism rushing through me. "And I really want to travel," I added, my voice light with my dreams. "And I guess, well, I want to live fully and authentically as myself," I finished.

Pete nodded. I thought I detected the ghost of a smile on his face as he drifted back to sleep.

There's nothing more powerful than a terminal illness to make us take stock of our choices. Something profound shifted in me during that conversation. What had seemed too complicated or impossible before, suddenly felt like actions I could accomplish, dreams I not only *could* but *must* fulfill.

As I sat beside my dying father, his body wasting away from years of hard living and neglect, I vowed to create a thriving, vibrant life I could be proud of. One filled with meaningful relationships, a fulfilling career, and opportunities to share my talents and passions with the world. My main priority was to become the best in my industry and achieve professional and financial success. This was mostly for self-serving interests. It would take becoming a mother, a cancer diagnosis of my own, and a global pandemic before I realized I wasn't the center of the universe. And that I could make a profound impact in people's lives as an expert in digital media marketing.

CHAPTER ONE

Atomic Life

· 1995 ·

PETE'S NEAR-DEATH inquiry wasn't the first time I questioned my life choices. A decade earlier, in the mid-nineties, I'd stepped out of the thick, smoky haze of The Atomic Cafe on the outskirts of Phoenix after a night of drinking, drugs, dancing, and fending off guys who would lead to the kind of trouble that I knew from witnessing my parents' tumultuous marriage wasn't remotely worth it. We'd reached that point in the night—or more accurately, early morning—where it was back to "reality." The house lights were about to come on, then the bouncers would herd everyone toward the exits. Instinct urged me to leave before that happened.

I coughed as I burst out of the tiny nightclub entrance into the chill of the dark, crisp predawn morning. The door banged shut behind me, abruptly cutting off the ear-bleedingly-loud music I loved because the high decibel level muted my chronic anxiety.

Atomic was a good forty-five-minute drive from home, but that didn't deter my girlfriends and me from making the trip several nights a week. Our fake IDs (I used my sister's birth certificate to obtain a driver's license that said I was over twenty-one, not my real age of eighteen) earned us entrance *and* alcohol, so Atomic was our go-to. More important to me, it featured the best live local bands and nationally known up-and-coming acts.

I've been obsessed with music ever since I can remember. It's provided the soundtrack of my life. Thanks to my sister, I was long past nursery rhymes and whimsical kiddie tunes by the time I turned six or seven. Kelley exposed me to the bands of the late eighties and early nineties, including Depeche Mode, The Cure, Yaz, and Erasure. Growing up, my appreciation for all kinds of music made me able to talk to anyone. Like a chameleon, I used music to create a common bond with just about everyone.

I also grew up on music videos. After my parents divorced the second time, my mother and I moved to Phoenix to be closer to family. Mom worked, and I watched *a lot* of MTV. I sat on the living room floor for three or more hours most nights, way too close to the TV screen, memorizing every single artist, title, label, and video director. I loved how every video told a story. Each one was unique and carried some message I could relate to my own life.

Music felt as necessary as oxygen. It brought me to life. When I listened to INXS on Kelley's double-cassette boom box or New Order on my Walkman, the music tuned out my constant fear of something terrible happening. That vague but looming terror accompanied me throughout an adolescence made even more tumultuous by my parents' repeated separation and reconciliation, two long-distance moves, and attendance at three high schools in two years. I never felt like I could depend on anyone to stick around or for anything to stay the same for long.

By the time I was a teenager, I *lived* for music. I flipped between rock, pop, and urban stations on the radio to catch my favorite songs, record them, and copy them to share with friends. I speed-dialed the song request lines repeatedly to make sure the DJs played what I wanted to hear. I made up fake names and disguised my voice to increase the odds of my requests getting airtime.

This love made Atomic so important to me. The club was an escape from my gnawing confusion and anxiety about life and how I wanted to live it, a feeling that grew stronger after I graduated high school. When I stepped inside the club, "real life" stopped existing. There was just the press of my body against others, all crammed into a tight space, swaying and dancing and singing and sweating together in the hazy darkness. I made most of my friends at Atomic. The club was like a cocoon. We all hoped that like caterpillars to butterflies we might somehow magically transform from angst-ridden teens and twenty-somethings into productive, successful adults without too much difficulty or suffering.

I'd spent the better part of the previous six months doing as little as possible. Disillusioned by the poor quality of instruction at the university where I'd started taking classes and with a growing apathy toward academics, I'd dropped out of college at the holidays. I spent my days working in a tanning salon, not exactly a career path to huge success. My life was mostly one big blur of a party at Atomic.

But the party felt over now. I shivered as I took in the dark windows of the closed businesses in the strip mall. The silence of the deserted shopping center boomed in my ears as loud as the music in the club. I turned and gazed at the shadows of the mountains behind me. For the first time, I felt directionless. I could no longer deny thoughts that had been creeping around in my mind for a while: Many of my friends were leaving the area to do other things. Even the owner of Atomic was moving on to open a second location in Austin, Texas.

I needed to decide who I wanted to be when I grew up.

A conversation I'd had with my paternal grandmother at Thanksgiving a few years earlier sprang to mind. Nana and I were in the living room, avoiding the chaos in the kitchen between my mother and my other grandmother. Nana and I didn't see each other often. I was furious with Pete for the way he treated my mom. The last time I'd been with Nana I'd unloaded my feelings about Pete to her. I judged him from my harsh teenaged perspective of black-and-white injustice.

Nana had responded stiffly to my rant. "He is still my son." She wasn't going to indulge me in bad-mouthing Pete. Recalling that last interaction, I felt uncomfortable sitting there with Nana until a song started up in my head. I was pretty well lost in the lyrics when it registered that my grandmother was talking to me.

"Huh?" I said, since I'd missed her question.

My grandmother took my lack of attention in stride. She leaned toward me. "I said, 'What are your plans for college?'"

It was the kind of stock question you ask a sixteen-year-old when you don't know them well enough to know their interests. But curiosity gleamed in Nana's eyes. She was genuinely interested in my answer. Perhaps this is what prompted me to respond with more than just a shrug or an "I don't know yet."

"I'll go to college somewhere," I said slowly, building up the courage to tell Nana the rest. "Eventually I want to move to California." I watched Nana's expression closely for signs of disapproval before I added, "I want to work at a record label."

My grandmother nodded thoughtfully. As a young woman she'd had dreams too. College-educated and fluent in Spanish and French, Nana planned to become an interpreter during World War II. When Roosevelt closed the banks, she put her grand plans on hold. Then she met my grandfather at a USO dance. They married and Nana raised twin boys, one of whom was my father.

Nana never fulfilled her career aspirations. I learned from her, as well as from my own mother, that nothing is more important than work. A job or profession meant money. Financial freedom. I wouldn't have to depend on a man or anyone else. The women in my life taught me, mostly by negative example, that it was crucial to support myself and not rely on someone else for my livelihood.

Nana reached out and clasped both my hands in hers. Her eyes penetrated mine as she squeezed my hands hard. "You must do it," she said with an urgency filled with the long history of her unrequited hopes and dreams, transferred to me in that moment as if from her hands to mine.

As I stood in the empty Atomic parking lot, peering at the mountains hulking in the distance, it suddenly dawned on me that, like the hills, my dreams were just out of sight over the horizon. College hadn't worked out, but that didn't mean I couldn't go after what I really wanted—to collaborate with artists and to understand how everything in the music industry works.

That night I wanted so much more than to listen and dance to songs that transported me into alternate states and realms. I wanted to be part of making music available to millions of other listeners like me out there in clubs like Atomic all over the world. Others who looked to great songs and videos to help them figure out life and how to live it. I found friends, comfort, and community through music. I sensed in my gut that there was some role for me in the music industry, a place that was rightfully mine for the claiming.

And claiming it was exactly what I wanted to do, no matter what it took.

CHAPTER TWO

It's Who You Know
· LATE 1990s ·

IN BUSINESS, who you know is often far more important to success than what you know. And the person with connections isn't always the most obvious choice. A stripper helped me land my first professional opportunity.

I'd always figured my life plan would one day magically reveal itself. In school, I'd been told that I was smart and talented and that I just needed to apply myself. I hadn't planned out how to chase a dream most people thought was crazy. I hadn't worked very hard, either, but the terror of getting stuck where I was, cleaning tanning beds and working in a coffee shop and getting annihilated with my girlfriends at Atomic Cafe, made me want to puke.

I didn't know the first thing about how to break into the music industry. But music was the one thing I was crazy about, and I couldn't imagine working at something without giving my heart and soul over to it. Atomic was my first "music school." I saw street teams doing DIY marketing and caught glimpses of how radio promotion worked. I got a taste of live- and recorded-music production. And I connected with other dreaming entrepreneurs who didn't find my desire to work at a record company ludicrous. I wasn't a performer. I didn't sing or play an instrument. I wasn't a songwriter or in a band. I wanted to know how people took a song and put all the pieces together to get it out into the world via radio, TV, print media, and so on. I ached to be involved in the music world at that level.

Sean, who I also met at The Atomic Cafe, was a drummer on the verge of becoming a prolific entrepreneur in the tattoo and body-piercing business. He urged me to check out a music conservatory where graduates were required to get internships in the music business.

I had my plan: If I could just get my foot in the door at a label through this training, I could really make a go of this dream.

This is where the stripper came in.

* * *

After I completed the program, I explored many official avenues to secure an internship at a record label. However, when Sean connected me with his friend Nikki, she made an introduction to her contacts at the Elektra Entertainment office in Los Angeles.

When I called her, Nikki got right down to business. "Here's the address. You'll meet with Mike when you get there," she said in a low, throaty voice that sounded tempered by endless hours in a smoky lounge. "Don't fuck this up," she warned. "I'm getting you in the door, but then it's up to you. They're going to think you're a stripper, so you better have your shit together and lead with your intelligence and passion. Don't make me look bad or make me regret doing this favor... And one more thing," she added, "always remember to help other people."

A career counselor couldn't have given me better advice. I took it to heart and made sure the people who interviewed me knew I was both smart and determined to make a meaningful contribution to the label, even in an unpaid position. They offered me an internship in the radio promotion department.

I packed my bags, said goodbye to everything and everyone I knew, and relocated to the Golden State.

* * *

The Elektra internship was unpaid. I temporarily moved into Pete's small house in Long Beach for a month. I hadn't been around Pete for a handful of years, and we were both uneasy about the arrangement, but I needed housing. Pete and I weren't close, but he tried in his own way to maintain our relationship. He liked to make me black coffee and an "Eggs McPete" breakfast sandwich before I left for the office every day.

Elektra ran at a frantic pace bordering on hysteria. I had to report to work daily at 7:00 a.m. The commute to Beverly Hills took two hours, which meant I woke at 4:00 a.m. every day, the same time I was accustomed to getting home during my club days before I became a productive member of society.

The full-time salaried assistants quickly trained me on my tasks. I was expected to be there first thing in the morning to turn on the lights, start the *one* department computer, fire up the fax machine, clean up if there there was any evidence of a party the night before, and pull reports for my three bosses, who often called the office on their way in to have me read them the data over the phone. Then I got their coffee or breakfast ready on their desks before they arrived.

Mike's order is still embedded in my memory: coffee with cream, hard-boiled egg, fruit salad, *cold* fruit punch Gatorade, and Marlboro Lights.

Promotion teams could work ten to fifteen songs at any given time, with countless other recurrents, multiplied by four to ten staff members. Each of my bosses called more than two hundred radios stations a week, promoting artists on the label from Mötley Crüe to Busta Rhymes. Each boss had huge binders filled with radio and sales data that we lived and breathed by. When new data came in via fax, I had to update the binders immediately. It was a lot of paper, hole punching, and highlighting, and a lot of white shirts ruined.

Recalling Nikki's advice to help other people, I made it a point to pore over all the data and make sure I understood everything. This came in handy when my bosses held meetings on how to promote the music. When they realized I was reading and analyzing the data as well as filing it, they listened to my analyses and sometimes seemed to appreciate my ideas. This made me want to work even harder to prove my value and worth to my superiors.

The team embraced and protected me. At nineteen, I was years younger than most interns, who were either in their last semesters of college or newly graduated. But they didn't go easy on me. It was like having a group of badass older siblings (all of whom spent plenty of time in the principal's office or grounded in their rooms). They made fun of me, made me do things over and over until I got them right, played pranks on me, taught me how to do grown-up drugs, and gave me tough love when I needed it. Most of all, they made me feel like I was part of a family for the first time in a long time.

Seeking out ways to help soon paid off. Once I proved I could handle basic tasks that I never felt were beneath me, which I found out later was a great advantage over other candidates, I was allowed to work the phones. Phone duty was holy. It was scary. We had to always get the correct name of who was calling, never get the lines mixed up, and never, ever let the phone go to voicemail.

Answering the phone was a full-time job, but I also had to pull reports, order meals, send gifts, pay bills, run expenses, greet people for in-person meetings, coordinate ticket buys, mail packages, run errands, and help with invite lists. My time at the tanning salon provided me with many of the skills I needed to manage my time and juggle multiple tasks. I knew how to answer a phone, track appointments, and make customers feel that they had my attention—that they were important.

Sometimes I didn't leave the office until very late at night. I made the two-hour commute back to Pete's and crashed into bed, then woke at 4:00 a.m. again the next day. I didn't do anything but work. It was hard, but I loved it.

My willingness to get my hands dirty on any task earned my superiors' trust and appreciation. This has served me incredibly well over the years. No matter who hires me, I try to have a servant's heart.

I was close to completing my internship and starting to worry about what I was going to do when it ended, when the office manager asked me if I'd like to interview for the receptionist position. I jumped at the chance. After months of working for free, I was beyond broke. Living in Los Angeles was expensive, and I couldn't afford much more than gas and food. I always found resourceful ways to live on a tight budget, a skill that's carried me through a lot of professional challenges. Taking a full-time job in the business felt much smarter than going into debt to return to college.

The fact that I wasn't twenty-one was an issue. Working for a record company required going to clubs and bars to listen to music. The assistants all hung out together, going for drinks and out to shows. Having an ambiguous job title on a business card meant you got free entry into most music clubs. While you might have picked up the dry cleaning and walked someone's dog that day, at night you were "someone who knows someone important." I had to be able to access the clubs.

During my interview, I assured the office manager I had it under control, then promptly took my fake Arizona ID to the California DMV and filed for a state ID.

I was Jennie during the day and Kelley at night. This was great for me for a couple of years until I turned twenty-one, but not so much for my sister. Once when Kelley was pulled over, she had a run-in with the law when two sets of state-issued identifications with her name came up, one with my face on it.

* * *

My first job came with a whopping salary of $19,500. Compared to the debt I would have incurred from college loans, I felt rich. I moved out of Pete's and rented a run-down, one-bedroom apartment across the street from the office. My roommate slept on a futon—the only piece of furniture in our living room.

I talked Rent-A-Center into taking Pete's credit card number over the phone in exchange for a used fridge and a mattress. We didn't have central heat or air-conditioning, a washer or dryer, or a dishwasher. The shower barely worked. The place smelled like mildew. But I had fucking made it.

Eventually I worked my way up from receptionist to assistant and sat back on the same desk I had hovered around as an intern. What a gift to come in and know exactly what I needed to do to be successful! However, the expectations were a lot higher. An intern was expected to deliver results on tasks provided to them. An assistant had to *anticipate* problems and opportunities before they happened and have contingency plans for all situations. My job was to make sure my superiors looked smart. That meant that I needed to outpace my bosses, all of whom had completely different styles and expectations of me.

Learning to navigate in multiple directions simultaneously was excellent training. I was overwhelmed a lot of the time, but my deskmates were my first professional teammates. We didn't let each other fail. I met assistants from other record companies too. A crew of us all hung out together, commiserated, and, most importantly, shared information about opportunities.

Work was my life. Looking back, I know I was hard to love, let alone live with. You know that friend who's a bad influence? Yep, that was me. My best friend from back home, Shelby, had moved to LA. I dragged her around the city to industry events even though she wasn't in the business. My dating life was sporadic and volatile. I felt disconnected from my friends in Phoenix. I wasn't good at keeping up with my family. My most committed relationship was with my job, which mattered far more to me than anyone in my life.

The music industry had two sides. By day we did business, but the nights were for partying. I was younger than most of my colleagues. Linde, one of my bosses, always went the extra mile to keep me on the straight and narrow. Whenever I started to drift down a wrong path, she redirected me. "Jennie, you're a smart girl," she'd remind me, using a tone only a mother figure can use. Sometimes her love came in the form of yelling at me. Sometimes she threw her Rolodex at me. (Google it if you're young and don't know what that is. They're heavy; that's all you need to know.) Sometimes it came in the form of banana nut bread, which she still sends me.

My time at Elektra provided an invaluable education and experience in the music business that I never would have gotten in a college or university. Every day, for twelve-plus hours, I observed the people around me and learned the music business in real time. They taught me life skills like budgeting, how to pay bills, how to buy a car, basic health care, and what guys to avoid (though they failed me there, bad). Elektra and my job were more than a career, a paycheck, and a community. They were my whole life. Which is why it felt like someone ripped my heart out of my chest when my next opportunity came knocking.

CHAPTER THREE

Trial By Fire

· LATE 1990s ·

WHILE I LOVED the music, my job, and my coworkers, at just twenty years old there was a lot more for me to learn about the industry. Elektra was a traditional company with HR policies and procedures and a very specific order for those who wanted to climb the corporate ladder. The next logical step up from assistant was to radio promotion representative. But there were no immediate openings in promotion, and a bunch of other assistants with far more seniority were in line ahead of me. No matter how much I contributed, my turn wasn't coming anytime soon.

I wasn't even interested in radio promotion. I hungered for experience in areas of the music business beyond what I'd been exposed to at Elektra. I wanted to know more about the creative process of how records got made, produced, and toured.

The late 1990s into the early 2000s was a strange time in the music industry. Change was thick in the air. Kids my age were no longer impressed by million-dollar music videos. They had stopped listening to the radio as frequently. And companies like Napster, with their peer-to-peer MP3 file sharing capabilities, struck fear in the hearts of radio salespeople and traditional critics.

I wanted to be on the cutting edge of where the business was headed. My boss Linde introduced me to her friend Stu Sobol, who needed a new assistant. The position meant a pay cut, but Spivak Entertainment was a thriving talent management firm. The company had divisions in television, film, and production as well as music. I wanted to understand the whole entertainment industry. My gaze set firmly on my future, I said a tearful goodbye to my friends at Elektra and moved over to Spivak.

Arthur Spivak was a successful executive and producer who represented talents including Prince, Tori Amos, and TV star Paul Reiser. He also produced the NBC hit show *Mad About You.* To my young and impressionable mind, Arthur was ahead of his time; he practiced feng shui and his wife taught Pilates long before most Americans had heard of either practice.

Stu Sobol was the antithesis of Arthur Spivak's controlled, unruffled demeanor. To put it in polite terms, Stu had a big personality, along with a booming voice that conveyed the passions of his big heart. Stu was a combination of brute force and street smarts that he leveraged on behalf of the budding musical artists he managed.

On my twenty-first birthday a stunning bouquet of roses arrived for me, compliments of Stu. He got up from behind his desk and came out to mine, where I'd placed the vase on full display. I thanked him and told him how much I appreciated the thoughtful gesture. He nodded, then his brow knit in the frown I had grown to recognize meant he wasn't happy about something.

"Count them." He waved a hand toward the flowers.

"Excuse me?"

"Count them." Stu huffed with impatience, the way he did whenever I didn't catch on to what he wanted fast enough. I was all too familiar with his groans and yelling. The culture at Elektra had been chaotic but it was managed chaos, with clearly defined responsibilities and duties. I had bosses and peers who explained processes and made sure I understood why things were done a certain way. There were forms to fill out, specific routes to completing tasks. I had expected that a management firm would be just as well organized and operated, but Spivak was far more like an entrepreneurial start-up than an established corpo-ration. If I saw something that needed to be done,

Stu expected I would do it without first being assigned to the task.

Young and inexperienced, I spent my early months at the company getting my bearings, using the well-honed observational and adaptability skills I'd gained from the multiple upheavals of my childhood to walk into a room and effectively deal with whatever I found there. I also continued to heed Nikki's advice and went above and beyond to help out anywhere I saw a need. But the fast-paced, adrenaline-fueled, "fly by the seat of our pants" atmosphere at Spivak frequently took me by surprise.

This time, Stu's directive was clear even if I didn't understand the motivation for it. I counted the flowers under my breath, then turned to him.

"Twenty," I said, before I could think better of what that meant.

"Son of a bitch!" Stu erupted. I winced as the words rang out through the office and my coworkers raised their heads to see who'd done something stupid to set Stu off yet again.

Stu ran a hand through his hair. "Get the florist on the phone!" he barked at me. "You tell them I ordered twenty-one goddamn roses and that they fucked up and came up short. And don't just accept an apology… Don't you dare hang up before they've given you a credit!"

I felt mortified and more than a little pissed that Stu expected me to call the florist and complain about my own birthday gift, but that was classic Stu. Quick-tempered and volatile, every interaction with him felt heightened. I met his big energy head-on. We duked it out in at least one, and often more, screaming fights a day.

Despite his larger-than-life persona, Stu also had a sweet side. I liked listening to the conversations he had over speakerphone with his two young kids most evenings. He'd ask about their days and tell them a funny joke or story, then promise to come in and kiss them in their dreams when he got home. I admired Stu as a father, even if I only got a glimpse into his parenting. It made me feel better about my own father. I wanted to believe that Pete was a good guy deep down, despite all his bad habits. Stu made me think that was possible.

I coped as well as I could with the office dysfunction and chaos, mostly by drinking, doing drugs, and staying out late even on work nights. I argued with Stu a lot. I took it personally when he yelled at me, even though he yelled at everyone and most of my peers didn't seem to care.

The longer I was at Spivak, the more resentful I grew. Many of our artists were around my age, too young and poor to afford a full road crew, so I was often sent with them to fill in the gaps. We came up in the business together and sometimes the bound-aries blurred; I was more like a friend or guide to them than a tour manager.

Despite my capability at managing our artists, Stu sometimes excluded me from important client meetings, even though I frequently helped with creative matters that went far beyond logistics. He made it clear that I was his assistant and that managing an artist on my own might not be in the cards. Under his tutelage, I didn't feel like I was learning "management" or any of the more creative components of the industry. Instead, I was expected to order lunch and coffee.

Still, I can see now that I learned a lot. I learned how to travel for business via air, bus, van, boat, helicopter... whatever it took. And how to keep a group of moving people on a schedule. I learned to advance and settle a show. I learned to never, ever leave the venue without the money. I learned how to activate a promotion and how to put an artist at ease. I learned how to deal with players, stylists, makeup artists, backup dancers, spouses (and sometimes "friends"), production crews, and hangers-on. I learned billing and receiving, along with the basics of record royalties and publishing. And I learned all of it because I wasn't told how to do any of it. I was just told to handle it. I was left to fail, got yelled at, was demeaned at times, and then was quickly sent back on my way to get results. In retrospect, this was a great gift. But it wasn't an effective way to learn. Later, when I decided to open my own company, I was determined to train my employees in a more humane, healthy manner.

* * *

One day about two years after I joined Spivak, I found myself praying the lights would turn red on the way to work so that I'd have a few extra minutes to myself. I cringed every time my home phone rang with a work question after hours. I sighed as I pressed the elevator button to our office suite. At just twenty-one I feared I had made a mistake. Maybe I wasn't cut out for the music industry after all. I blamed my circumstances instead of taking responsibility.

On another day, like any other, after yet another blowup, I couldn't take it anymore. I quit on the spot without another job lined up or any kind of backup plan. It felt bold and good… for about five minutes. Then I was disappointed in myself and my actions. Although my instinct to leave was right, I reacted without thinking it through or creating an exit strategy. If I had just given myself five extra minutes and planned out my next move, I wouldn't have been sitting on my couch wondering how the hell I was going to pay the rent.

CHAPTER FOUR

Joining The Mickey Mouse Club

• EARLY 2000s •

I SPENT THE next few months at loose ends. Dissatisfaction gnawed at me. I had to get a job, but since I'd left Spivak impulsively, my next position was likely to be a lateral move instead of a strategic step up the career ladder. I landed back at Elektra as a temporary employee. I felt sheepish every time I thought of Linde, who had put her reputation on the line when she recommended me to Stu. I imagined she might be mad at me for leaving Spivak.

The unsettled feeling continued. I left Elektra for a position with an independent radio promoter, but that wasn't fulfilling either. I still wasn't sure who I wanted to be or what I wanted to do, so I was working just for the paycheck. I second-guessed myself constantly. Perhaps I'd made a mistake by dropping out of college. I hid my fear of the future by pretending I was in the movie *Swingers*. I drank and did drugs until even partying started to feel stale.

Just as I had nearly convinced myself to go back to college, I landed a position at Disney's Hollywood Records as the assistant to the head of promotion. This was a dream come true. After the roller coaster of working in the entertainment industry, the stability and highly structured environment of a large corporation were alluring. I longed for the clear expectations and boundaries of a role that included a formal orientation, a job description, and regular performance reviews. I missed having someone like Linde mentor me and look out for me.

Disney felt like a fresh start. I had learned from my past mistakes and was highly motivated to take control of my career again. Hollywood Records was a soft place to land. Unlike the resentful rebel role I'd played while working for Stu, at Disney the lure of job safety was so strong that I adopted the persona of the "good girl," the one who would do anything to move up the well-established ladder. I was still too young and naive to understand that the corporate promise of job security and guaranteed success, if I did what I was told, wasn't true.

Soon enough, I grew frustrated with the monotony of being an assistant. This was particularly difficult because I poured so much time and energy into my job. I was now in my mid-twenties, growing up and maturing. Since I wasn't partying as much anymore, I suddenly had a bunch of empty hours in my schedule. The trouble was, I didn't have any hobbies, nor many people in my life outside of my coworkers. I didn't keep in touch with my family much. It just wasn't a priority then.

I did have the support of the community. Los Angeles was filled with transplants like me who had moved there to pursue careers they still believed in while the rest of the world deemed them unattainable and unrealistic.

While there were like-minded dreamers around me, and I kept in touch with some of the other assistants I'd worked with at Elektra and Spivak, my best friend Shelby had moved back to Arizona. Most of my other friendships faded as I focused on my need to become someone "important" before I reached my thirtieth birthday.

* * *

Just like in my career, I unwittingly felt determined to follow the rules in my personal life. Driven by a self-inflicted desire for roots, I had boyfriends, but I blew through them and quickly left them in the dust. Having my own place and my independence was as important to me as stability. It said I could make a living and support myself in LA, where the cost of living was high.

By the time I was at Hollywood Records, I had moved in with my boyfriend, a good-hearted, wild-child drummer who I'd met in a bar. Pepper was funny and smart, and with his laid-back, laissez-faire attitude he didn't appear conflicted about my ambition.

I could be demanding and dictatorial, a real bitch, when I felt like it. I was no picnic to live with, but Pepper and my friends tried to love me. I wasn't interested in marriage in my mid-twenties, but my agenda of proving to myself, my family, and the world that I could successfully "adult" included checking that box.

* * *

Something I enjoyed about my time at Disney were the changes that popped up in the industry with the advent of the internet. As the online world grew, so did illegal downloads of music and videos, and phenomena like Napster. The Walkman turned into MP3 players. MTV gave way to watching videos online. It was an exciting moment to be in marketing, a turning point away from traditional avenues and into tech offerings.

I fell into the de facto demographic of consumers for the online realm. My bosses often sought me out for insights into how and why young consumers were accessing products online. Suddenly I felt like a hot commodity instead of a lowly admin. As the music marketing business changed, I rode the wave, savoring the return of some of the thrill I'd felt working at Spivak, but this time with some solid ground under my feet.

Despite the new innovations in the industry, for the most part my duties felt routine and mundane. I might have stayed at Disney a lot longer had I been considered for positions with more responsibilities.

The last straw came when the Detroit local radio promotion director position opened. Instead of considering me as a serious prospect, the higher-ups offered the job to a woman who sent in her résumé in calendar format. Each month featured suggestive photographs of her in different outfits—scanty Valentine's Day red satin shorts, a cheesy Santa costume in December.

I took this as a sign I needed to focus on what I wanted to do next. What showed up when I put out feelers about a job change was something I couldn't even have begun to imagine.

CHAPTER FIVE

Big-Girl Pants

· EARLY 2000s ·

MIKE WEAVER, a former coworker at Spivak Entertainment, turned me on to a position at Yahoo!, where he was now employed.

"Yahoo! has acquired a CD-ROM magazine and media company called LAUNCH," he explained when he called.

"Mike, I'm a music person, remember?" I cut in. "I know less than zero about working in the tech industry," I reminded him dryly.

"This *is* the music business, Jennie," Mike countered. "We're on the precipice of an on-demand

69

world. And the position encompasses everything you've learned. We have all the tech resources we need," he explained. "What's missing is a music person... someone who understands sound and programming and how it all comes together for marketing. That's why we need you. Trust me. You gotta go for it." Mike sounded far more enthusiastic about my abilities and the position than I felt.

While Mike saw what I could bring to the company in terms of experience and my potential, I didn't look great on paper. I was a college dropout who'd had four or five jobs in the five years I'd been working. Anyone reading my résumé would think I was a wild card. So my first interview with Yahoo! turned into five more to prove myself.

From my perspective, the online audio streaming technology that Todd Beaupré and Jeff Boulter had built at LAUNCH was based on the listener-experience standpoint from day one. That set it apart from the other new-to-market competitors trying to build an online alternative to radio.

As the development and algorithms became more robust and intuitive, programming got more complicated. Todd and Jeff had great respect for the artists and the songs that powered their product. But the technology and the artists never felt more important than the listener. Unlike traditional radio, where a show host chose songs and commercials played almost as frequently as music, Todd and Jeff's technology allowed the listener total control over what they listened to and when. I appreciated this about the two bright, driven young guys.

It took a massive amount of follow-up and convincing before Jay Frank, a vice president in the department, finally offered me the position of music director for what was then called LAUNCH and later renamed Yahoo! Music.

After all the rigamarole around landing the job at Yahoo!, I was still lukewarm about taking it. I liked the cachet of working for Disney, a known and well-respected company. And I felt some trepidation about the buzz around layoffs and plummeting stock values at Yahoo!, AOL, and similar organizations.

I didn't want to leave Disney, but I feared I wouldn't get the opportunities I wanted there. I loved the people, the culture, and the movie lot environment with its hustle-and-bustle atmosphere. I could have made a lifetime career there, been financially stable and secure. Unfortunately, I hated my job.

Joey, the head of rock promotion and one of my superiors at Hollywood, gave me the pep talk of a lifetime in the alley behind our building one day when he discovered me chain-smoking cigarettes and brooding over whether to leave. Joey wasn't the kind of guy you talked about your feelings with. He was the guy you called when you needed hockey tickets, reservations at the current hot-spot restaurant or club, or a stripper. But he came through with the perfect perspective that day.

"You'd be crazy not to take this opportunity. You're getting a raise, stocks… All the signs are there that it's a great deal. It's a bold move to go from being in the music business to working with the internet," he said. "But that's just like you, Jennie! You've got more balls than most of the guys around here." Joey made a wide, sweeping gesture at the building behind us. "This is exactly what you've been training for! Put on your big-girl pants and take the goddamned job at Yahoo!"

By the time we went back inside, Joey had me convinced. Just as my grandmother had told me that I must go after my dreams and ambitions, Joey confirmed that despite my doubts and fears, my future was waiting for me not at a record label or an entertainment promotions agency like I had assumed, but rather at a cutting-edge company that was making history in the tech and music realms. I was not going to be a music businessperson working in the US. I didn't know it at the time, but I was about to become a content person with an opportunity to create a positive, healthy digital world.

CHAPTER SIX

Yahoo!

• EARLY 2000s •

EVEN THOUGH YAHOO! was a well-known entity, the music and entertainment portals were still in their infancy. "Legal" entertainment across the internet was new and was accompanied by the feeling that anything was possible. I've heard it aptly described as the Wild West.

I don't recall having much time to get up to speed in my new job. One day during my first week in the Santa Monica office, I sat in a meeting at a long conference table, watching Todd Beaupré scribble on a whiteboard.

I stared hard at what Todd was writing. There were so many lines, arrows, and acronyms. My head spun as I tried to make sense of what my mind read as gibberish. I blinked a couple of times and then looked around the room at the young, highly educated technical staff mixed with seasoned and respected industry people, as well as fire-starters from all different walks of business. Suddenly, I understood. Dave Goldberg and Bob Roback, the founding partners; Todd; and all my other new colleagues in that meeting were forging new paths, not following well-worn trails to success. To succeed at Yahoo!, I would need to be proactive in my strategies. It wasn't up to my colleagues to speak "music business" to me. It was up to *me* to understand the internet business, be passionate about how our platform worked from the inside out, and eloquently express metrics of success (or failure).

That night I bought a new notebook, then returned to the conference room. I copied down everything Todd had written on the whiteboard. I carried that notebook with me every day. Anytime there was a word, symbol, or acronym I did not understand, I learned about it. I filled the notebook in no time. It sat on my desk for years as a reminder that it was my responsibility to keep learning and to stay up to date on the most current industry trends and advances.

There was so much innovation happening *to* the industry instead of the industry *creating* innovation that, for the first time, the fans and consumers were driving the trends. What carried the heaviest weight of all? Word-of-mouth recommendations from friends.

Up until this point, the content owners pushed a limited amount of product out into a limited number of places, concentrating on radio, TV, and magazines. But with the internet, a limitless amount of content was in the pipeline, circumventing the mainstream industry. Every day it seemed there was a new website, a new player, or a new place to get music news. It was a race to be the biggest and best. It was also a time of great fear as the difference between legitimate music websites and peer-to-peer, illegal networks were not always clear. The recording industry sued hundreds of computer users, including dozens of college students, accusing them of illegally sharing music across the internet.

Yahoo! was sought out as an exciting venue to promote and grow music careers, but we also faced lawsuits and the very real threat of being shut down. Some days it felt like we were on top of the world. Other days, we were accused of single-handedly ruining the music industry. It was painful to be picked on for trying to push the traditional systems into the new age. We had to defend the company and explain repeatedly that we weren't killing businesses and careers; we were creating a new space for artists to connect with fans.

All these years later, as I think about what Dave and Bob created, I am just as in awe as I was when I showed up bright-eyed and ready to change the world. They were far ahead of their time, and they don't get the credit they deserve for establishing some of the fundamental foundations that much of the music business is built on today.

* * *

In my early days at Yahoo! I worked with my boss, Jay Frank, and my closest colleague, Brian Marshall. Jay was highly accomplished for a thirty-year-old. Jay was more than a boss; he was a mentor. Articulate and intelligent, he wasn't afraid to speak his mind, but he always did so respectfully. He didn't let me rest on my well-rehearsed college-dropout routine. I wasn't allowed to blame any shortcomings on my youth or inexperience. He pushed me to make sure I addressed both the creative side of things and the analytics, since data determined our success.

My coworker Brian was just a little older and more experienced than I. He was tall and mellow with a calm demeanor that, along with his jeans-and-T-shirts wardrobe, made him approachable even though he was well put together and handsome. Brian had a strong work ethic. His peacemaker attitude frequently defused my quick-to-ignite indignation and fury. He'd remind me with a lopsided grin and a shrug of his shoulders that we had a fun job, we were all wearing a lot of hats, and we'd let a lot of people down if we didn't dig in and do the work. Brian and I laughed a lot. Our small department of three moved along happily for a couple of years.

One day Jay called me into his office for my employee review. After I sat down across from him, he looked me right in the eyes. "Jennie, you've overdelivered on all of your goals this year," he said.

I smiled, pleased. Nikki's advice was still paying off. I was making decent money, receiving stock, and having fun along the way. I felt pretty good about things.

"You're undeniably passionate about your job, and you have great instincts coupled with a competitive edge," Jay continued. My smile expanded as I sat up straighter in my chair. "However," he paused meaningfully before he continued. "I'm going to be brutally straight with you. At times you come off as an abrasive know-it-all."

I blinked back hot tears, furious at myself for letting Jay see that his words were getting to me.

"There's no need to be so combative. You gotta play the long game, Jennie. Especially now. I need to know I can count on you to manage effectively."

I nodded and fought back a sniffle. Our department of three was about to merge with a team of twelve others from a newly acquired company. Jay expected me to oversee the new people, a very different role from the one I'd been playing mostly on my own.

"I want you to repeat after me," Jay said. "More accepting, less reactive."

I nodded but didn't follow along, fearing I'd burst into tears.

Jay repeated the phrase until it became a mantra. I can still hear him saying it in my head.

He gave me the tools I needed to grow into an even better, more effective leader. But all I heard was that I wasn't good enough, and I wanted to argue with him. I felt like I was being picked on.

I went back to my cubicle and cried, not because I was sad, but because Jay was right. My reaction to his feedback proved the point—despite being good at my job, I was immature. If I didn't have the ability to train others and grow talent, I wasn't helping scale the business. I needed to grow up and, as Joey at Hollywood Records used to say, put on my big-girl pants and adopt a positive and encouraging team mentality.

Despite Jay's "pep talk," when the new people joined our department, my initial reaction was to play defense. How was I going to keep all my duties, all my stations, all my labels, all my genres? Most importantly, how was I going to keep my position behind Brian? What if a new team member came in with more experience? What if I didn't like them? What if Jay or Brian liked one of them better? What if I wasn't the best in my field, like I always wanted to be?

As rapid-fire insecure thoughts raced through my brain, I took a big breath. No one was taking anything away from me. We were getting additional resources and talent so that we could grow. That was a profound step toward maturity for me. For the first time, I let my experience and logic win out over my insecurities. I did as Jay told me and repeated his "More accepting, less reactive" mantra. For a minute, I embraced it.

This was a good thing because with the new staff coming on, the only place where the creative and editorial teams could office together was on the ground floor. The building had a beautiful studio where artists recorded our content, a cool kitchen, plenty of bathrooms, and windows that let in a ton of light. But when you walked beyond that area, before you entered the massive library of audio CDs and videotapes, there lurked a dank, oversized hallway just large enough to house the fourteen of us. It was so dark our eyes literally had to adjust to the light whenever we stepped outside, which we didn't do often because we were ridiculously busy.

Brian and I were used to sitting in close quarters. Probably more times than Brian would like to remember, I wheeled my chair over to his cube and sat next to him while he fixed all my problems. But now we had twelve more people we barely knew jammed into incredibly close quarters. We all bitched about who we were sitting next to, how we could hear them chew their food, how loud they typed, and even questionable personal hygiene in some circumstances.

But for the most part, the transition to a department five times larger in size went well. There were more people to divide duties among, which took some stress off me and Brian. I took Jay's suggestions at my performance review to heart and made an active, conscious effort to be more communicative and inclusive in my decision-making, to become more of a team player than a lone-wolf badass. And even though we had a big department now, I still depended on Jay and Brian the most.

* * *

I had been at Yahoo! around three years when Jay called me into his office for a meeting. This time the news was even harder to take than my performance review.

"We're creating a new leadership position," Jay began.

I figured the new role would go to me or Brian. By then, we had become the number-one global music service, so I thought we had done a pretty good job. I wanted it, but Brian had more seniority and experience. I'd be happy if it went to him; he had earned it.

Instead, Jay said, "Jennie, we've already identified our candidate. He comes with extensive radio experience."

I recoiled in shock as if Jay had hit me. This must have been a hard decision for Jay, and I know he made it based on the needs of the business. But I couldn't take my perceived injustice of being passed over for someone who I didn't think had near the amount of firsthand knowledge and passion about our platform I had worked long and hard and gone above and beyond to accumulate.

John Lenac, the new hire, was a perfectly nice guy. He provided me a layer of protection and reinforcement, and we worked quite well together. But I couldn't swallow my fury and resentment at his presence as my new boss. I was at a dead end at Yahoo! and was, for the first time in years, open to new opportunities.

I had learned enough to know better than to quit without lining up another position first, but fueled by my anger and desire to move on, that didn't take me long. The last straw came when my home was broken into. Suddenly I found myself wondering what the hell I was doing in Los Angeles. Within months, I was ready to leave not only Yahoo! but also the city where I had done what I'd dreamed of doing all my life: establish my career in music.

CHAPTER SEVEN

Bless Your Heart

• EARLY 2000s •

"This is all my fault." I was talking to Pepper, who was sitting in the window seat next to me, but I spoke loudly, and my tequila-slurred words echoed around me. Several of the other passengers on the early morning flight from Los Angeles to Nashville swiveled their heads around and glared at me as if they completely agreed.

"Tia is obviously your fault," Pepper mumbled without opening his eyes. He had fully reclined his seat and shut his eyes as soon as we were airborne. Apparently, this somehow allowed him to also shut out the screeches rising from beneath my feet where Tia, who I can only describe as a feral asshole, protested in her carrier. The cat hadn't stopped yowling since we'd boarded.

Images of my beloved pit bull Lola emerged from the alcohol-induced fog in my mind. Tears brimmed as I imagined her down below with the other flight cargo.

I had been all business in the days leading up to our move. There was plenty to do even though my new employer, Warner Bros., was paying for the movers who packed us and loaded the truck. But I had lost my carefully crafted composure when I handed Lola over to the cargo crew. Suddenly I found myself wondering what the hell I was doing. Was it really a good idea to quit a great job and leave good friends, and even Pete, who I saw every few weeks for dinner and walks or bike rides on the beach, to move somewhere I had only visited once? I wasn't so sure anymore.

My decision to move to Nashville was equally

influenced by hitting a career ceiling at Yahoo! and my fuck-it philosophy that I applied to everything that sounded interesting, including a new hair color and jumping out of a plane. And also by the notion I carried, as I think many young people do, that by the age of thirty I had to be "someone," doing "something important." Getting married, having a career, and buying a house in the suburbs were all crammed in under a looming self-imposed deadline.

The second-guessing clamored even louder when one of the flight attendants announced that we were making an emergency landing in Oklahoma because a passenger on board was having a diabetic seizure. Surely that was an ominous sign, meant to tell me how screwed I was. Suddenly I felt trapped by my own decisions.

I glanced over at Pepper, who didn't move or even make a face as the plane banked and then descended toward the Oklahoma City airport. Part of me had been hoping that when I announced I was moving to Nashville, Pepper would decide to stay in LA and we'd break up, clean and easy. That way, I wouldn't be the bad guy. Instead, he was willing to come along for the ride and adventure of it all. He was fully committed to our relationship. I wouldn't admit that I wasn't.

My doubts skyrocketed after we finally landed in Nashville. The airline personnel lost my dog, and by the time Pepper and I shepherded a bewildered Lola and a furious Tia into a taxi, we were all strung out on travel, stress, and exhaustion.

As we rode in the cab, I took in the chain restaurants and strip malls that made up the landscape around our corporate apartment, which was located thirty miles south of the city in a quiet suburb that felt nothing like the bustling, crowded neighborhoods of LA. Between the haze from the tequila and the surreal sense that lingers after air travel transports me from one locale to another, I felt as if I were in a suburban dream. Stepford, perhaps. Pepper and I were unlikely to fit in well with the neighbors.

That night when I went to the Publix for

groceries, the cashier asked for my ID before she rang up my beer. She looked at my driver's license, then up at me.

"Are you really from Hollywood?" she asked as she peered at me through the same large-framed glasses my grandmother wore. She looked about the same age as my grandmother too.

"Yes, I am," I said.

She shot me a big smile. Then she said the three words that you must avoid having used against you at all costs when you live in the South: "Bless your heart."

* * *

I signed on at Warner Bros. Records, even though I'd said I would never work for a record company again. However, country music lagged way behind other genres in digital growth. The opportunity to make a lasting digital footprint for an entire genre was too tempting to pass up.

I wasn't an expert in the genre, but after I was assigned to manage it at Yahoo!, I fell in love with it. Country was gritty and dirty and real, all the things I appreciated about all the music that had ever inspired me. What I loved more than anything was the storytelling of the songwriters. I was also impressed by the artists' willingness to work hard. It was very different from the rock scene, which was filled with a lot of pretension and privilege. Country music artists genuinely appreciated those of us on the business end of things, and it felt more like an equal collaboration between creatives than the rock scene, where the artists were encouraged to believe that they were the most important people in the room.

The vibe at Warner Bros. was much more corporate than Yahoo!. There were processes to learn, forms to fill out. And a hierarchy that was striking in comparison to the collaborative philosophy evident even in the open-floor-plan-and-cubicles layout at Yahoo!.

The office space on Music Row was split between floors and departments. More often than not, doors were closed. For the first time, I had an office of my own. I didn't like sitting in it by myself. I missed the diversity at Yahoo!. I wouldn't say I was longing for the basement, but I wished for a happy medium.

My pal Lynette Garbonola and I were the new media department. Bill Bennett was our boss. We were a progressive team, seeking innovative ways to grow our audience. Bill gave us a long runway and sometimes strategically turned a blind eye to what we were doing. He often said, "You're going to do *what?*" Everyone would be together in a conference room, going around the table, sharing their latest win or plan. Bill would take his glasses off and look at us for what seemed like a *very long time*. Then he'd either laugh and say "That's great!" or he'd ask us if we were out of our fucking minds. For the most part, both were correct.

At the time, country music was still almost solely relying on country radio for promotion. Even our digital marketing campaigns were targeted to capture the country radio listeners' information, particularly their email addresses.

Lynette and I were able to deftly navigate between most departments. We had a hand in creative, marketing, sales, and promotion, which brought a lot of variety to my workdays. Almost everyone at Warner Nashville wanted to help drive the digital movement forward, including the artists with whom we tried a lot of different marketing tactics.

Our digital strategy included onboarding and maintaining networks with Friendster and Myspace; asking the very few country music blogs to review our albums or songs; asking AOL, Yahoo!, and MSN to include our music in their programming; counterpart digital promotion on the few broadcast channels in country music; and inclusion in the download stores.

It was a much simpler era in terms of licensing and permission, but a horrible time for creator compensation. Legal on-demand streaming wasn't readily available. We either had to purchase a limited quantity of downloads or ask for free licenses to administer the promotions.

We worked with our partners—artists, radio stations, print media—to ensure their websites and other marketing materials included opportunities for listeners to sign up, and we watched the information trickle in. It was exciting. For the first time, we could identify who our customers were and keep in touch with them. It was all a gamble, one that took the sign-off of the artist, the manager, the label's legal, and the publisher. Not easy, especially in a town full of publishers and songwriters who believed everything started and ended with radio and anything else was going to kill their career.

The first time I came face-to-face with a publisher who wanted me to quantify the value of giving a download away for free, I was scared. I wasn't sure how to measure the value of capturing a listener's email address or zip code or how to quantify the value of establishing a direct relationship with listeners. But I felt passionately that while we might be missing a $1.99 sale, the potential to earn an authentic relationship could bring us far larger returns than one transaction.

I had to look a lot of people in the eyes and tell them it was going to be okay. I had to ask them to trust me. That weighed heavily on me. I was uplifted by my team, who supported the experiment and brought their artists and repertoire (A&R) and promotion expertise into the fold. We also had a great lawyer who listened to an idea and thought of all the ways we could execute it rather than leaning into all the reasons we shouldn't.

We spent many hours debating the permanent influence of country radio. Radio was the be-all and end-all for success. Artists banked on the money they could make once they hit a chart position. Digital was growing, but the two didn't yet see eye to eye. I became very outspoken—not only internally but externally on panels and interviews—explaining my belief that by growing a new audience, we weren't taking away from an established one. I believed passionately in my position and had never been one to back away from a heated argument. However, it came off as me trying to disprove the validity of radio, which didn't make me popular among my more traditional peers in the industry.

* * *

My habit of making work my whole world didn't change when I moved to Nashville. Despite the self-imposed domestic goals that I had unwittingly adopted from the popular culture around me, I was far more wedded to my job than to my relationships. It got most of my time and energy. Just like in LA, I prioritized ambition and career success over personal relationships and friendships. While I occasionally kept in touch with my friends in Phoenix, as the years passed our communications fell off. I met my need for connection through my interactions with work colleagues, most of whom shared my zeal for the music business.

Pepper and I continued to drift apart too. We'd had a wedding in Las Vegas, but forty-eight hours later I stood out on the balcony of our honeymoon hotel room and said to my new husband, "I don't know if we should have gotten married." He hadn't taken that so well and came back with something predictable, like, "What the *fuck*?"

I now know I was desperately seeking a "normal" life, according to rules that didn't apply to me. Whenever I tried to figure out what would truly make me happy, I envisioned a romantic partner, and even kids. My parents' marriage and others from their generation had shown me what I *didn't* want. And sometimes I feared that without a positive role model, I'd never be in a relationship that prioritized individual and collective growth for myself and my partner. I wanted and needed to create a fulfilling, joyful life based not on societal dictates but on my own terms.

CHAPTER EIGHT

Getting a Clearer Channel

• EARLY 2000s •

WARNER BROS. LURED me from LA to Nashville, but soon another company came knocking on my door. When Peter Harper first explained to me what his group at Clear Channel was trying to accomplish online, I didn't want to talk to him. I heard "Clear Channel" and immediately dismissed it as terrestrial only and antiquated, far out of my wheelhouse. Peter patiently explained about the new programs they were building, including plans to rebrand an entire digital ecosystem under the new iHeart moniker. He also indicated his boss, Evan Harrison, had headed up the team at AOL (Yahoo! Music's main competitor) prior to moving to Clear Channel.

The idea of learning from Evan and Peter was more enticing than the job itself. Given Evan's experience at AOL, I would learn a lot about my previous competitor under his leadership. Marrying that knowledge with what I knew about Yahoo! would benefit me, whether or not I succeeded at Clear Channel. It seemed like the odds of success were in my favor just from learning what Peter and Evan could teach me. I accepted the newly created position of director of content and marketing, a role that put all my previous experience and leadership ability to the test.

If there was ever a music genre in need of a company like Clear Channel to close the gap between terrestrial and digital, it was country music. My department's primary goal was to help country music listeners bridge that gap. Our fresh new branding initiative encouraged listeners to expand their current habits of listening to Clear Channel at home and in the car to listening on their computers (and eventually their phones.) Our platform and content programs were well received externally. What I did not account for was the opposition I encountered from within the organization.

Clear Channel was a large company with offices all over the country. I worked out of the local Nashville radio cluster office. My direct boss was in LA and the rest of the digital marketing team members were in New York and Cincinnati. The New York office was fancy and fast-paced. I was very excited when I had the chance to meet everyone there in person. The progressiveness and talent of the entire division impressed me. They all came with a heap of experience I had not been exposed to and ideas that I probably wouldn't have considered had I not worked with them. The climate was stressful, but the corporate structure at Warner Bros. had prepared me for that.

My division, with strong leadership from Peter and Evan, set forth a very aggressive growth plan. One of my duties was to introduce our new "digital manifesto" to some of the highest-ranking terrestrial radio programmers in the business and share what we were going to do collectively on the national level.

The local programmers often weren't as jazzed as I and the New York team were about these changes. Several old schoolers at the company did not want our division's help to ensure that their digital repertoire was congruent with what was happening in the world. Already behind the times compared to other media conglomerates, we had made great strides in the basics of websites and emails, and we had the most beautiful audio and video content shoots (thanks in part to a very spunky and creative force, Mitchell Stuart). At this point, social media consisted mostly of Facebook and Twitter (now X). Most of the stations ran their social media locally, and the brands were busy and inconsistent.

Many of the programmers felt threatened by our directives. One accused me of taking food off his table by taking the focus off terrestrial radio. From my perspective, I was saving his table since terrestrial radio was dying and we were providing another source of revenue that was growing exponentially. But he just couldn't see it from that vantage point.

In retrospect, I understand why I was met with a few cold shoulders among our local programmers, the good old boys. I had done a lot of poking the bear regarding the ongoing legitimacy of radio in the past. The programmers probably didn't perceive my announcement about the growth plan as the collaboration it was meant to be, but rather saw it as a forced directive from corporate (even worse, from New York City).

For the first time, people wanted me to fail. I felt a lot of pressure to forge a path for others coming up behind me in the industry. And I recognized that there was a glass ceiling.

I had a male colleague send emails I drafted

about programming initiatives, as I felt they would be better received and implemented if they were delivered by someone other than me. I told myself this was a good business decision based on getting results for the artists who had committed to be part of our programming. The discrimination was more generational and "local versus corporate," but it was sprinkled with sexism too. I had numbers to hit. I was determined to make some of the unenthusiastic non-adopters successful online despite their self-constructed roadblocks.

Thankfully, I had the support of three people in the local Nashville radio station office, which I worked out of when I was in town. The two on-air personalities Big D & Bubba, along with Keith Kauffman, the station program director, helped me understand the radio industry so I could create more effective content for digital media.

When I'd been working for Clear Channel for about three years, Pete called. I noted the time, which was after 9:00 p.m. Odds were good that Pete was drunk. He had to be, to ignore my rule about phoning only in the morning.

I had set strict boundaries on the communication I accepted from Pete. He called me three or four times a week before I left for work, when it was still well before dawn on the West Coast. I'd learned from experience that if I talked to him at night, he'd be wasted.

I picked up anyway, certain I would regret it.

I was right.

CHAPTER NINE

After Hours

· 2007 ·

"WHAT IS IT?" I asked through gritted teeth when I answered, anger so close to the surface that my face flushed.

"Jen," he said, his baritone voice muted to nearly a whisper, "I'm in the emergency room."

"What did you do?" I bit back exasperation as multiple scenarios filled my head of Pete being arrested for a DUI, getting into a fight in some gloomy bar, or having a domestic spat with one of his many girl-friends, whom he kept track of by first name only in a tattered pocket-sized black address book.

I imagined him wincing and struggling to sit up in the bed. "I'm not healing from the goddamn hernia operation I had last week. The people in this hospital are telling me that I need to be patient because I'm old. I told them this isn't my first fucking rodeo. Something is wrong, but the goddamn HMO has me talking to a bunch of admins instead of doctors. I'm in a lot of pain. I just want to go home." His voice trembled. The vulnerability in his words pierced me. At sixty-six years old, Pete was still athletic and tough. He rarely complained about his health.

I jotted down the hospital information and then ran across the street to my neighbor Ana. She and her husband, David, were the only friends I had outside of work. Ana was a nurse. If anyone could help, it was her.

After I told her about the call, Ana sat me down at her kitchen table. She picked up the phone and dialed the number of the hospital.

"This is Jennie Smythe. I'm calling to get some details about my father, Pete Smythe, who's a patient there…" Ana pretended to be me. Her authoritative demeanor soothed my jitters as she asked question after question. I could tell from the one side of the conversation I overheard that Pete was dealing with something more significant than a post-op complication.

Ana thanked the hospital personnel and hung up. Her typical warm smile was gone, replaced by a somber expression. She walked over to one of the kitchen cabinets, opened it, and took down a bottle of Jack Daniels. She filled a glass a quarter full of the rich amber whiskey, then set it down in front of me.

As I raised the glass and took a sip, my neighbor met my questioning stare with a stiff nod, her lips pressed into a tight, thin line. "You need to get on a plane."

* * *

I took Ana's advice and spent a week with Pete while he underwent multiple tests, most of them inconclusive. Pete had beat colon cancer earlier in his life. Detected during a routine colonoscopy and successfully removed surgically with no need for chemotherapy or radiation, it was the best-case scenario for a cancer diagnosis. This time, though, wasn't another near miss. Pete had incurable pancreatic cancer.

Pete wasn't advanced enough for hospice yet, so he remained in his tiny place near the beach and went to the ER anytime he had a health issue. Since the cancer wasn't treatable, the health-care staff suppressed the pain with pain meds and sent him home. On days when he felt well enough, he went to the store, rode his bike on the beach, and played golf, even though the meds made him feel out of it.

For three months, I flew between Nashville and Los Angeles, sometimes twice a week. Pete lived far from LAX, and the commute was brutal, but I did it. Thankfully my Clear Channel team was supportive. They helped me work remotely as best as I could

with the technology available at the time. I kept a
BlackBerry and a laptop for work and a separate
phone for personal use.

On one trip back to LA, I went to see Pete at yet
another hospital that his HMO had relocated him to
in the middle of the night. I had only gone home
to Tennessee for a couple of days and was shocked
at the days-old beard on the old man. I gasped in
dismay before I could catch myself. I had never seen
Pete with hair growth on his face. He was militant
about grooming and organization. He made his bed
every morning and kept his closets and drawers tidy.
Regimented even in his addictions, he restricted his
drinking and smoking to nights only. And he was
always clean-shaven.

I recall him from my childhood, wandering
around the dark house in the early morning hours
in his underwear, shaving with an electric razor. No
matter how late he'd been out the night before or
how hungover he was, Pete was always up, dressed,
shaved, and caffeinated by 6:00 a.m.

Pete was embarrassed about his condition now.

I was pissed. "What is going on, Pete?" I asked him.

"No one here speaks fucking English." He tried to sit up.

I glanced over at the elderly man in the bed next to Pete's. He nodded hello, as if to reassure me he didn't mind Pete's cussing.

As I reached over and pulled the curtain between us to give us all some thinly veiled privacy, I silently mouthed to the man's wife, who was hunched in a chair next to his bed, "I am so sorry."

She smiled at me, put her hand to her chest, and mouthed back, "It's okay," which was kind and generous, two things I was starting to believe didn't exist in the Los Angeles hospital system.

I turned back to my father. "Pete, when did you eat last?"

"I'm not hungry," he muttered.

I bit back a sharp blast of resentment. My anger came and went unpredictably, and I struggled to keep it from erupting. "I know, but the doctor said if we can't get your weight up, you can't have chemo. You must eat."

He didn't argue with me. He knew I was right. He also knew the next step was a feeding tube, and he wouldn't do that.

"I'd like some Jack in the Box French toast sticks," he said after a few moments.

I grew worried when the French toast sticks went uneaten. The nursing staff and I got Pete cleaned up after I threatened to sue. While Pete dozed in clean sheets, I pulled out my laptop to catch up on work, which was always on my mind.

Pete's roommate's wife left to get some dinner. The orderly came in to bathe the man, who was in so much pain he begged the aide to come another time when he felt better.

The aide ignored his pleas.

Since the man's wife was gone, I couldn't help stepping in. "The man said he's in pain!" I shouted at the stubborn aide. "Don't you hear him? Bring a doctor in here and get him some relief!"

I understood then why the wife never left her husband. I didn't feel okay leaving Pete while he was in that facility either. Traveling back and forth made it nearly impossible to keep on top of everything between visits.

Pete began an opiate regimen to counter the pain, and we lost all control of the situation. He couldn't stay on top of his medication. I feared he was going to overdose. Whenever I was back in Nashville, Ana called the facility and tried to talk to a nurse over the phone for me. However, the quality of care was poor and often inhumane. Pete was in chronic pain and frequently inconsolable.

For nearly fifteen years I had fantasized about leaving Pete to die alone as payback for all the hassles he put me through, all the times he was loaded and embarrassed me, all the events he never showed up for, all the lies he told. I imagined how satisfying it would be to know he got the end he deserved. Now here I was, understanding for the first time that this time with him was a gift. By extending grace to my ailing father and forgiving him, I was giving myself grace too. I wanted as much time with him as I could get.

CHAPTER TEN

BiTTeRSWeeT FaReWell

· 2008 ·

ONE NIGHT, I sat alone in Pete's apartment, trying to work and get a few hours of sleep before I went back to the hospital in the morning. I felt agitated. My marriage had ended, and I was living alone again. I was distracted by the stress of flying cross-country frequently, trying to keep up with my job duties and care for my dying father.

I got up from my laptop and paced the tiny studio. My mind moved through moments with Pete over the past few weeks. We had shared some nights in his apartment. I made us frozen lasagnas and bagged salad. I helped him to the bathroom, made sure he took his medication as directed, and tucked him into bed before he drifted into an uneasy sleep that usually lasted two to three hours. Then we repeated the routine.

What I couldn't grasp was how a man who was once a wealthy, successful oil executive with a wife, kids, and a nice house had ended up isolated in a small apartment with only a few grand in the bank.

Pete pretended that he had chosen the beach-bum lifestyle because it was cool. But we both knew he was out of control. After a few poor investments, a tumultuous personal life, and several pending lawsuits, he was in a bad downward spiral. None of his affairs were in order. This was no way to end a life.

I twitched with grief and anger. How could he have let everything go?

A framed photograph displayed on an end table caught my eye and my heart. It was of me and my older sister, Kelley, as young girls. Despite not having the two of us in his life in a meaningful way for many years, Pete kept our childhood pictures all over his apartment. We were proudly displayed like his greatest trophies.

I snooped through Pete's drawers that night. I read his calendar and address book. My entry was a page of old addresses and phone numbers crossed out above my current one in Nashville. My birthday was written in bold and underlined, surely a result of his paranoia from forgetting my birthday once when I was a teenager.

The longer I paced the small room ruminating, the more I craved some kind of escape, something to release all the pain, hurt, and anger coursing through me and making me jumpy as hell. I recalled a moment just before I left the hospital that evening. Pete had thanked me for being there. "I love you," he'd added. He'd been telling me that a lot lately, nearly every time we were together. Despite his weakening tone, his failing body that was diminishing faster and faster between my visits, I had answered the way I always did: "Okay."

The memory cracked my heart wide open. A sob built in my throat, but I willed it down again. Instead of giving way to my grief, I raced to the cabinet where Pete kept his booze. I grabbed the one remaining bottle, unscrewed the cap, tilted my head back with my mouth wide open, and upended the bottle. The little bit of alcohol left in it burned a blazing path down my throat.

I moved into the bathroom, where I stared long and hard at the sleeping pills and antianxiety medication in the medicine cabinet. I reached out a hand, longing for relief. It would be so easy to take some pills and check out for a while.

I yanked my arm back and stumbled out of the bathroom, ashamed at the sharp, insistent temptation to gobble down the meds. In my twenties I'd indulged to the point of having an undeniable habit, but I had steered clear of recreational drug use for a couple of years.

I was so scared my stomach hurt. I sat down on the living room floor, clasped my arms around my knees, and sobbed. "I can't take anymore," I cried aloud to God. "I can't do this!"

I poured out my heart and soul as I prayed for help. I'd been trying so hard to hold it all together, to be there for Pete, to work and act like I had it under control, despite the small voice that whispered incessantly in my head, telling me I wasn't strong enough. I confessed that despite all the gains Pete and I had made in our relationship, I was still mad at him for abandoning Mom and Kelley and me when I was a girl.

The pressure in my chest lifted. My racing mind eased to quiet calm. For the first time in my life, I felt a strong, distinct external love and support that I couldn't explain. I brushed it off initially, but throughout the next months that sense of being held or contained returned whenever I asked it to. Each time, I was comforted, strengthened, and given everything I needed to keep carrying on.

That higher power brought physical support too. My older sister hadn't seen Pete for a decade, but for some reason, she had felt compelled to call him right before he got sick. Now Kelley came to the rescue so we had coverage for Pete when I couldn't be there.

After hours on the phone with shitty insurance companies and even shittier doctors, we got Pete into a rehabilitation center in Hollywood that had a competent, caring staff. Linde, my former boss from Elektra, generously opened her home to me and Kelley. She provided us with comfort and a maternal care that soothed us when we felt weary or demoralized.

We were able to get Pete's pain under control. By the time he was ready for release from the rehab center, we felt confident that he would be fine at his studio for a couple of weeks until we figured out the next move. There were chemo regimens that could extend his life, and he was finally at the point where we thought he might put on enough weight to tolerate the treatments.

Pete went home, but a few days later he side-swiped a bunch of parked cars in his VW van while driving to the pharmacy to fill his prescriptions. He was taken to the rehabilitation center in Long Beach and soon was on a steep decline. The facility started hospice care. Pete stopped picking up his cell phone, and getting through to him on the hospital phone was harder than it should have been. Thankfully the hospice nurse called us daily with updates.

This was around the time Pete asked me the question that profoundly changed my life: *"If you knew your life was half over, what would you do with the rest of it?"*

Pete made amends in his own way by asking me that question, and by talking with my sister, Kelley, as much as she would allow. He called our mother and told her she had done a good job raising us despite his absence. He told Kelley and me stories that I didn't recall hearing before. We remembered times when we were happy together, and things that Pete did to make us strong. We laughed.

Pete was still a huge pain in the ass, and I threatened to leave him a hundred times. But he apologized, and I knew he meant it. He had regrets about how much of our lives he had missed out on. He really wanted to meet his only grandchild, Kelley's daughter, Ava. He knew he was dying, and for once he tried to make sure we knew he loved us.

My thirtieth birthday fell on Saturday, March 8, 2008. I had plans to celebrate in Nashville. I'd fly back out to California the next weekend. But when my phone rang around four that morning, I knew it wasn't someone wishing me a happy birthday.

It was a nurse from the rehabilitation center. Pete was gone. My sixty-seven-year-old father took his last breath on my thirtieth birthday, making it crystal clear that he hadn't forgotten the day, and putting his Pete stamp on it to make sure I didn't forget the motivation to live my life fully.

Kelley and I met at LAX and made our way to Pete's apartment. As we walked inside, I stopped in stunned shock as I took in the wood-block calendar on the shelf. It was set to March 8.

Pete hadn't been in his apartment for several weeks. I was the only person who had been there. I pointed this out to Kelley, and her eyes widened. We couldn't figure out how the calendar was set on that date. Perhaps it was a last nudge from him that he was okay with how his story ended.

Kelley was also surprised to see photos of her daughter on Pete's refrigerator. She didn't know that I had been sending pictures to Pete for years. My sister blinked back tears as she took in Ava's likeness at varying ages from infancy up to her current age of three. Even though he never met his granddaughter, Pete had displayed every single picture I sent of her.

Kelley was insistent about seeing Pete one last time before the cremation. I didn't want to, but like most times in life, if Kelley told me to do something, I did it.

There he was, lying on the table: tan, handsome, full head of hair. My sister stroked his head, tears falling from her eyes. She said, "You did the best you could." Kelley had made her peace with him, and by that time, I had peace too.

Right before Pete passed, he said he wanted his ashes scattered at his favorite places. His friend took part of him to the ocean and part of him to the golf course. The rest of Pete's ashes are with me. One day, Kelley and I will get on a chairlift together and let him go in the mountains. One last run with the girls who know he loved them, which is truly the only regret I think he was worried about dying with.

CHAPTER ELEVEN

LIVING THE DREAM

· 2008 ·

I STAYED TRUE to the dream I had shared with Pete to go into business for myself and to make a positive impact in digital media. Shortly after I returned to Nashville, I went straight to my boss, Peter, and told him I didn't want to renew my contract with Clear Channel. Jay Frank, who had also relocated to Nashville and provided solid and sturdy (and sometimes tough) counsel, gave me a pep talk in advance. He reminded me that I'd fulfilled my three-year contract and given the company my all; I didn't owe them anything more.

Yet after all Peter and my team had done for me over the months Pete was ill, I felt nervous about disappointing them. I was also anxious about the risks of opening my own business. Leaving a solid salary with relative autonomy to create a company from scratch wasn't something sensible people did. And it certainly wasn't on my radar when I started out in the music industry. The idea of being my own boss and leading a successful team really appealed, though. And the prospects at the intersection of art and commerce were electrifying. Social networks were exploding with opportunity, and someone needed to be the team captain. I decided that could be me. I strongly believed that I had a mission to accomplish.

After several months of half-hearted attempts to salvage our marriage, Pepper and I had gotten a divorce. I was single again. I didn't have kids. I had moved into a new house closer to town. I had no debt. As painful as the previous few months had been, it felt like they had set me up at the perfect time and with the perfect mentality to take a risk. Yet when I told Peter "I want to start a digital marketing agency," suddenly the idea seemed a lot more naive and unreasonable than it sounded in my well-rehearsed inner dialogue.

Leaving Clear Channel taught me how to depart from a role in a professional manner. I wanted to be sure that Peter, Evan, and the team knew how grateful I felt. I supported and guided my friend Allison, who was stepping into my position. My departure from Clear Channel serves as the model for how I want to feel when I leave projects and how I want my employees to behave when they move on to other opportunities.

I didn't have a business plan when I founded Girlilla Marketing in 2008. At the time, it was nearly impossible to know or predict what marketing might look like in three to five years. My "plan" was to help artists successfully navigate the marketing terrain while making enough money to pay my bills. If it didn't work, my fallback was to get another job. For the record, over fifteen years later, that's still my plan.

My first priorities were to land a few clients, get health insurance, and save enough money to hire a teammate. Early steps toward reaching these goals were simple and straightforward. I purchased a new computer, set up a checking account for the business, and brought on several interns eager for experience in the industry, even though that meant working out of "office space" I rented in an attic on Music Row.

In 2009, blogs were becoming more mainstream but were often looked down upon by the traditional media world. I was happy to work with them. Myspace was still a force then. Facebook wasn't yet the marketing behemoth it is today, but it was growing. YouTube was providing all the Susan Boyle and Obama inauguration videos our hearts desired. Twitter was having its moment as communication king.

While the surviving networks look much different now, the biggest hurdle wasn't rights, monetization, or marketing. It was understanding and harnessing the ability to communicate directly and unfiltered with followers/friends instead of via a manager, agent, or publicist. Removing the buffer that handlers, critics, and journalists provided in the past was both a tool and a torch. Now all users had the power to log on, read reactions, and join in a universal conversation in real time. One negative comment from a random follower could tempt an artist to react online emotionally without fully understanding how that could potentially add fuel to the fire of criticisms.

The first year of business was full of wins and losses, hard lessons, bonehead decisions, celebrations, and sleepless nights. I was accustomed to long hours and working hard, so there wasn't much adjustment there. I set up a rotation with the interns that provided almost around-the-clock digital triage for our clients. Clients could call, text, or email day or night and we'd help with their digital marketing needs and quandaries. Our reputation quickly grew. In no time, we surpassed the modest monetary goal I had set so that I could hire and insure my first full-time employee.

Ashley Alexander, my lead intern and later a freelancer for Girlilla in the last stretch of her days as a music business major at Belmont, was quite possibly the most put-together young person I knew. Ashley is smart, funny, dependable, and understood the music business. She also took out the trash without being asked to do so (shout-out to her parents for raising her well!).

Ashley represented pretty much everything I wasn't, *and* she was fun to be around. From the jump, she had my respect, and she still does today. I seek her counsel or opinion on most matters. I joke that ours is the longest committed relationship I've ever been in.

We were plugging along nicely when I experienced my first major setback, courtesy of the health insurance industry. I felt that having full employee benefits would change our image from being a "freelancer with freelancers" to being a real and scalable company. At the time, there weren't many people doing what I was doing, especially in

Nashville. But I wanted the company to operate with all the solid business practices I had benefited from in my prior roles.

Girlilla Marketing wasn't big enough to have a small-business insurance policy, so I applied for individual plans for Ashley and me. These plans were expensive, but I didn't care; it was the right thing to do. I still don't consider insurance a business cost. I view coverage as an investment in my most important asset: my team.

My first mistake was telling the truth on my health insurance application. When I was traveling relentlessly, I often suffered from sleeplessness. As preventative care, I got prescriptions for sleeping aids and antianxiety medication, which I took responsibly. I disclosed that.

I also disclosed a brief, horribly misguided stint on lithium when I lived in LA. A psychiatrist I'd seen for help around my recurring anxiety and family history of alcohol dependence had prescribed the heavy-duty medication after just a single thirty-minute consult. After several months of living in a listless fog, barely functioning, I weaned myself off the lithium and never went back to that doctor again.

Nearly ten years later, after I moved to Nashville and was trying to shoulder my family and work responsibilities, I sought help for what my primary-care doctor called situational depression. I explained to her that I had sleeplessness and problems with travel and time zones. I was upset over Pete's decline and burning the candle at both ends. I felt confident that if I could get my sleep under control as I had in the past, I could remedy the situation. My doctor sent me to a psychiatrist, who gave me a sample of an antidepressant that would help with sleep, anxiety, and depression.

I took the sample one night, woke up the next day, and was so out of it that I nearly crashed my car on the freeway. I never filled the prescription, but I disclosed it as part of my medical history.

I was now labeled with a mental illness, a

preexisting condition. Every insurance company refused to cover me.

I wrote to the insurance company, pleading my case. My primary-care doctor and psychiatrist wrote letters on my behalf, explaining the situation in detail. Unfortunately, the psychiatrist sent my *entire* file to the health insurance company. It included confidential session notes about my past, my father, and other unnecessary details. I felt so naive, and tremendously violated by the medical community.

This, combined with the stress of starting a new business, put me into full panic mode. There was so much I didn't know about running a business, but I knew that I needed to keep myself healthy at the very least. Around this time I met Tatum Hauck Allsep, who helped me navigate our health insurance options.

Tatum later founded Music Health Alliance (MHA). I am forever in debt to her and am now a proud MHA board member. She also referred me to a psychiatrist who helped me manage my situational depression. I was able to get to the root of many issues and clear out some old beliefs so that I could make room for God's plan for me and my mission around shaping the digital media landscape for clients in the music industry.

I would like to wrap up this part of the story with a bow on top. But the reality is that I didn't have any pretty options. We devised a solution that temporarily gave me what I needed (including some peace of mind) and allowed me to concentrate on the business, which was starting to take off.

CHAPTER TWELVE

Searching Abroad for My Legacy

· 2009 ·

AFTER GIRLILLA had been open for a year, we had about a dozen musicians, actors, and brands as clients. There was room for more, so when a friend told me I should meet with the CEO of Average Joes Entertainment, a new record label from Georgia, I agreed. Average Joes's flagship artist was Colt Ford, a white rapper cowboy who moonlighted as a golf champ. I was so intrigued by that descriptive mash-up of styles that I spit my coffee out.

My interest in Average Joes was piqued, but

Shannon Houchins, Average Joes's CEO, seemed disengaged and uninterested when we met for coffee. He acted aloof as he offered vague glimmers of what he was doing and his vision for his company. I felt annoyed at wasting my time and countered by telling him all about Girlilla Marketing in highly animated detail. I didn't hide my ambition or desire to become known as an expert in the digital marketing field. Pete's question still came to mind at least once most days, and I did my best to live up to my career goals.

Shannon and I eventually warmed to each other professionally, and he brought me and my team in to work with Colt Ford. As I got to know Shannon better, I grew impressed by his inventiveness. He was highly intelligent and articulate, and I quickly realized his eccentricities were representative of his incredible creativity. He just didn't communicate like anyone I knew. We worked well together, and soon I found myself looking forward to our calls and meetings.

Another introduction that proved fruitful was to Matt Maher, head of the Nashville office for a talent management company called ROAR. Almost immediately, Matt struck me as someone special. He had a clear vision for the company, and his management style was deeply ingrained with his musicality. He knew the creative side of the business inside and out, crucial for both recording albums and in live production. He also held an optimistic outlook on the future of the industry. I was used to getting pushback whenever I talked about digital music, but Matt didn't flinch. I liked him, and he seemed fascinated by what we were doing at Girlilla Marketing.

Our companies quickly fell into a symbiotic operating relationship. We served the same clients in different roles. We were working on so many projects together that soon Matt approached me about buying Girlilla Marketing. It was a very tempting proposition. Girlilla Marketing had made a lot of progress, but it was still in the fragile beginning stages of a new business. We hadn't branched very far out of Nashville yet.

ROAR offered me support on the parts of the business that were a significant burden. The idea of being able to remain at the helm of the Girlilla Marketing ship but have help with the back office, insurance, and capital for talent acquisition was extremely attractive.

Could I build on my own what they were offering help with? Even if it was possible to do so, would I succeed a lot faster with additional resources? These were questions I drove myself nuts pondering late at night as I went 'round and 'round in my head, trying to forecast the future and arrive at answers.

Finally, I did what any smart CEO would do. I made good on another one of my promises to Pete and hopped on a flight to Europe for two weeks, leaving my newly graduated employee, Ashley, in charge of the business so I could clear my head and make a decision.

* * *

Getting on a plane for a solo romp through Hungary, the Czech Republic, Austria, and Slovakia was a real adventure. I had only been abroad once before, when I'd gone to Italy a year earlier with my friend Kelli after we drunkenly swore we'd go. Both of us were too stubborn to back out.

One of the more memorable events of that trip happened after I got bit by nasty Italian mosquitos in Florence. I left our hotel room to get calamine lotion and Benadryl at an all-night pharmacy. It felt strangely like buying drugs for an after-party—I rang a doorbell, a hand came out of the wall, I put my cash in the hand, and I was given an unmarked bag with the medicine.

Now, I boarded my overnight flight from JFK to Budapest, found my seat, and took my Ambien. Rookie mistake. Just as I was getting that warm feeling of sleep coming my way, we had a technical malfunction and had to return to the gate, deboard the plane, and wait for the mechanics. I bought a huge coffee and refused to sit down.

Eventually, we reboarded the plane. I zonked out, and when I awoke, we were descending. I felt like I had entered an eastern European twilight zone. Everyone and everything were impossible for me to understand.

A voice announced on a loudspeaker in multiple languages that all North Americans were to go left and everyone else was to go right. The Canadian sitting behind me explained that no, we weren't being held hostage as sex slaves (like the recent blockbuster film *Taken*). We were being screened for swine flu. The Hungarian people wanted to make sure we didn't have it or spread it.

After a couple hours in quarantine, they sent me on my merry way to explore Budapest. I had no plans, no phone, no friends to talk to. It was just me, my notebook, a promise to Ashley I'd check in with her once a day via email, and my thoughts.

I knew that if I created space for myself, the answers would come. But first, I had to uncover the right questions. To do that, I needed to see a bigger world than my own. I needed the pressure of death, Pete's question to me, and the promises I wanted to make for the futures of those I loved. For too long, I had drawn everything that I needed from inside myself. Now I was hoping for guidance. I had moments of fear and loneliness, but also exuberance and precision.

I wandered. I wrote. I went to museums. I walked in parks and markets. I drove to Vienna and did more of the same. That was followed by a brief visit to Slovakia and a few days in Prague, where I spent time in awe of the history and the beauty of a faraway land that didn't seem so foreign anymore. As I walked and toured the cities and towns, I contemplated my future.

What would I want to accomplish if I knew my life was half over? What did success look like to me?

After just a year in business for myself, I felt fantastic about the services I was offering and the caliber of my creativity. I wanted to hire a small team as soon as possible to build on the momentum, but

I did not feel comfortable going into personal debt to do so. I was on my own as a new businessperson without any track record or the kind of business plan that banks like to see before they hand out loans and lines of credit.

In my unplugged eastern European adventures, I acknowledged to myself that I needed to concentrate on marketing, not back-office duties. I needed capital to hire staff, and that staff needed the benefits packages they deserved. By joining a larger firm, I'd gain a built-in set of advisers (that included three lawyers) who had a vested interest in Girlilla Marketing's success.

In Prague, I walked along the Danube until I reached a park with a statue of Franz Kafka, author of *The Metamorphosis*. I was contemplating the kind of legacy I hoped to leave behind someday when it hit me: My heart believed I could build the business on my own, but I'd build it faster and with fewer obstacles if I had the support ROAR was offering me. I needed to shift my perspective from feeling less like

I was losing my freedom and more like I was gaining the means to bring my vision to life.

By the time I returned from Europe, I was ready to sell. The acquisition terms were simple. I would maintain partial ownership. I would work with ROAR's clients for internal credit, and ROAR would help me get more clients. We'd all grow together in our collective business. The ROAR partners assured me that I would have autonomy, which was the most critical element. My company wasn't worth anything on paper at that time, so there wasn't a monetary transaction to write home about.

However, *I* was valuable. I wish I had understood my value to their business during negotiations. Over the next handful of years, working with my partners—who all brought strong often conflicting voices to the table—taught me how to better express my value and negotiate effectively. Eventually I relied upon that wisdom when I had to negotiate against them.

CHAPTER THIRTEEN

Setting Down Roots

· 2010–2011 ·

OWNING A BUSINESS is like falling in love and being broken up with every day. Every twenty-four-hour period has the potential to be thrilling, to envelop you in passion, to make you feel one hundred feet tall. It can also disappoint you, making you feel betrayed, bewildered, and taken advantage of. What sets a *leader* apart from a *boss* is that you come back to work the next day, ready to love again and give it your all. You cannot afford to do otherwise.

I returned from Europe inspired and excited about the possibilities for the future. Gone were the days in LA when I hoped for red lights to delay my arrival at the office. I was eager and ready to grow the company and see just what it—and I—might become, and what kind of impact I could make on digital marketing practices.

After the acquisition announcement, the five Girlilla team members and interns crammed into one small office and hallway of ROAR's three-office suite. While it was a step in the right direction from the attic, we didn't have parking, we constantly blew out the power source, and it was impossible to take a phone call or a meeting (or a pee) without everyone knowing the details.

It was not an option to have clients visit Girlilla Marketing at this location, so we spent a lot of time traveling and holding meetings in other venues. We had one phone line, and we all had to be extremely quiet when it was in use, which caused a lot of uncontrollable giggling. Through this intimate experience—not unlike my basement time at Yahoo!, which I really loved deep down—I forged a strong bond with Ashley and Stevie Escoto, who joined us in 2010. These two amazing women had the same kind of work ethic and attitude about helping that I'd learned from Nikki long ago. Both are still at the heart of everything we do.

Girlilla Marketing's first key hires came from different areas of the music business. Our greatest strength was melding traditional marketing and promotion, technology, publicity, and publishing. Employees have come and gone over the years, but the core group ensures that we continue to apply our experience and common-sense approach to the new landscape. I cannot expect it to stay this way forever, but I know how valuable each team member is individually, and I also appreciate the value of our collective chemistry.

New interest in our services increased beyond our expectations over the next few years. Scaling a business like Girlilla is complex. The number of clients on board dictates the number of employees and hours needed to service them. But more clients do not necessarily equal more profit. The business doesn't always grow with volume. My terror of missing an opportunity created more friction than saying no to monetary growth.

When it comes to taking on clients or employees, there are very few perfect fits. When you find one, you know it deep down. Everything else is a waste of time—or worse, a double waste of time, as it generally takes at least a year to get dead weight removed, and then you're back in the same place where you started. Over the years I've learned from experience to take care when I select clients. I'm even more cautious about the employees I hire. There were a few times I was afraid to turn down new clients and made some poor hiring choices just to have the manpower needed to meet the demand. I also kept employees way too long out of loyalty, even when they blatantly demonstrated their inability to evolve. I soon regretted those decisions. I've learned to stay open to expansion on all levels, but not at the cost of the team's quality.

When we joined ROAR, we acquired a few of its marquee music and talent clients, which gave us new global visibility. In the past, we were usually brought in after the major creative decisions were made and only assigned limited, specific tasks. Now we filled seats at the table in the planning stages of albums, films, tours, and television shows. It was an exciting time to be on the ground floor, planning for the next five years (which is like fifteen in digital marketing years). We learned a lot about the parts of the business we weren't historically involved in. And we offered insights into the future landscape of the market, which influenced some of the creative pathways, for better or for worse. To me, it felt like we went from cramming into an office and tripping over one another's computer cords to celebrating hearing our name on a Grammy Awards telecast in the blink of an eye.

The night of the awards ceremony I was home alone, watching it on TV. A buzz of excitement and delight ran through me when one of our clients—a band—included Girlilla Marketing when they shouted out their thanks after they won a Grammy. A moment I'd dreamt about for a long time had finally come true.

People in the business know how much time and effort it takes to create something worthy of a prestigious award. My family, and most of my friends who weren't in the industry, didn't really understand what I did for a living. While they didn't completely know what it took to win, the award conveyed a certain cachet. My client's Grammy win was definitive validation that we were on the map.

Soon all of us at Girlilla Marketing were running in all directions and having a blast. Almost every day we got a call about a new opportunity that was too good to pass up. We pitched a lot of things we didn't get awarded those first few years. However, just being in the room and meeting people was the real opportunity. In a lot of cases, we made connections that came to fruition much later.

With new clients in Los Angeles and New York and ROAR primarily based in both cities (as well as Australia), we racked up airline miles flying between offices to meet our new coworkers, pitch new clients, and reestablish relationships with platforms and outlets that did not yet have a presence in Tennessee.

As we took on more clients, we also expanded our offices to include Los Angeles and New York. That was a mammoth blunder. I allowed the pressure of "needing someone in LA" to dictate hiring for location instead of hiring the right talent for the job. I didn't want to spend much time in Los Angeles, so I opened an office with three people there and assumed they would run it as I would. Wrong. I soon discovered that if wanted the offices to run the way I ran things, I needed to be there. Things ran exponentially smoother when the staff was all in Nashville under one roof. I closed the New York and Los Angeles offices less than a year after they opened.

* * *

While business moved on a strong upward trajectory, my personal life unexpectedly did the same. Shannon Houchins and I forged an unlikely friendship not only as client/vendor but also as business owners. Soon we shared several mutual clients.

Shannon had a small office in Nashville, but he was still based in Athens, Georgia. He was also scaling quickly and spending more time in Nashville. When he suggested that I rent a portion of the new office they were opening, I jumped at the chance to finally have our own space.

The more we got to know one another, the more I liked and appreciated Shannon. An extraordinary blend of intellect and creativity, his talent, smarts, and ingenuity captivated me.

In addition to growing my business I thought I might want a family. I did not want to repeat the pain of my parents' marriage. I longed for a true partnership, one in which we felt like equals.

Shannon wasn't shy about making his romantic feelings for me known. While I was interested in pursuing a relationship with him, I had been groomed my entire career not to date people I met through business. I felt the pressure of all the unspoken double-standard "rules" that still affect women and our professional reputations. An affair can be a high five for a man and a career killer for a woman.

It was a confusing time for me. I was drawn to someone who I respected and felt on equal footing with. But we were also connected professionally. Should things go south, it would be a big blow to my team (and potentially embarrassing), and a logistical nightmare to separate offices. Most importantly, it could affect Girlilla Marketing's fragile bottom line.

But the more time I spent with Shannon, the more I felt like we had the potential to be two individuals in a thriving partnership. He was often the first person I called in the morning and the last person I spoke to before I went to sleep. For once in my life, I could talk to someone about every aspect of my day. Since Shannon was also in the business, he understood how hard it was for us to gain traction in our industry, and he was genuinely happy for me.

Our time together allowed me to combine my passion for my career with my personal life, instead of feeling like the two were mutually exclusive. Shannon never resented how much time I spent at work. He wasn't intimidated by my independence, which allowed me to soften and be more vulnerable because I knew I could trust him. He became my closest confidant on all fronts.

I began to take emotional root in Nashville, expanding my crew with a new rescue dog, Claud Von Dog. For the first time since childhood, I felt that I had a place. A home.

One night I sat across my dining room table from Shannon, working on our separate business endeavors. We'd spent most nights that I could recall in the recent past like this, both of us engaged in our passions with zero pressure to stop working to meet the other's needs or expectations. The profound respect that had started in our professional partnership carried over into our blooming personal relationship too.

Talk turned to our hopes for the future. When Shannon told me that he understood my ambition and wanted to see me grow to meet my dreams, I realized that I didn't want to let go of the special bond between us. The reward was worth the risk. I am grateful he was confident and patient and waited for me to come around.

Not long after, we discovered that we were collaborating on another project. I was pregnant, expecting in August 2012. Shannon and I married in 2013. While marriage and family hadn't come to mind when Pete asked me what I'd do if I knew my life was half over, as everything fell naturally into place for me and Shannon, it felt like a blessing beyond what I'd ever been able to imagine.

CHAPTER FOURTEEN

Motherhood and Media

· 2012-2016 ·

I never wanted to be a stay-at-home mom. I was too passionate about my work. I'd put a lot of time and effort into building Girlilla Marketing. The company was my first baby in many ways. I also recalled all too well how much my mom struggled after Pete left and how screwed she was financially. I was never going to let that happen to me, so financial independence and autonomy were huge priorities for me.

While I didn't want to abandon my career to have kids, motherhood made me contemplate the contributions I was making to the world. Becoming a mom made me want to do my job even better. I believed that our industry's primary objective was to entertain, communicate with, and connect people in healthy, vibrant ways that enriched audience members' lives. I wanted to protect and support not only the musicians who were my clients but also the consumers on the other side of the screen.

This grew more and more challenging from 2010–2020. During that time, the content and scope of the digital space exploded far beyond what I imagine the platform pioneers originally envisioned the World Wide Web would become.

Email marketing, while still important, became less of a way to communicate and more of a way to highlight merchandise and other monetizable content. Mobile devices made a mainstream debut. Suddenly everything we did needed to be done twice to meet the different requirements for both desktop and mobile usage. Social media shifted to user-generated content, giving way to a new host of challenges (and newfangled platforms) in terms of rights and monetization. The technology mutated so quickly that we found ourselves communicating much more frequently with lawyers and business managers. There were more hoops to jump through, more hands in the pie, more opinions to wrangle, and much bigger consequences. As the "Friend," "Like," and "Follow" buttons appeared, fans and users could watch the rising success of their favorite artists, and our work became more quantifiable and manipulatable.

Digital marketers worked tirelessly in areas that had been traditionally handled by niche experts in content creation, copywriting, sales, publicity, customer service, crisis management, rights management, advertising, and all the correlating analytics. Sadly, we still faced skepticism over whether social media or digital marketing were important. Sometimes people were angry we even existed. We were dismissed as an afterthought (or worse). We were often placed in a position of defense and having to justify ourselves, rather than being embraced and given the assets, tools, budget, and talent we needed to be successful. Early in the decade, we at Girlilla Marketing developed a strong spine and a willingness to hold our tongues, even though we knew we were right.

Marketing always has been—and is always going to be—selling a product. There's no such thing as an entertainment medium or platform that isn't selling you something. It may not be a direct sell at times, but it's a sell, even if it's building an audience to sell something to later, or somewhere else, or a thought or suggestion of how you should look, live, and be. After I became a mother, it felt important to help create a digital world that was safe for my kids.

Suddenly the stars of the platforms were the people using our content, not our clients or the content itself. I've seen a lot of trends come and go, but none as vapid as the influencer. Influencers are the pyramid scheme of social media. What a strange left turn we took, from raging against big-box retail and traditional commercials, to paying for premium streaming to avoid commercials altogether, to then willingly connecting to glossy, peculiarly similar-looking talking heads saying things like, "Well, sis… this is *ah-mazing*. Let me put you on to this thing you don't need that has *changed. My. Life*."

Consumers trusted influencers, only to discover that it was all a big commercial. Once these influencers had to start disclosing #ad or #sponsored, we were surprised that these perfectly curated creatures might not be posting about these products out of the kindness of their hearts but rather because they were getting paid to do so.

Disclosure was a nice first step to remedy "dirty advertising" and a way for the social media sites to pretend that they cared about their end users. However, aside from a few public Kardashian-type shamings, getting "busted" has not been something to fear. The platforms are expert at indemnifying themselves, so they have no real responsibility for anything that gets created or communicated on them. This hit fever pitch with politics in 2020 and got even more exposure thanks to great documentaries like *The Social Dilemma*.

There are other drawbacks to the rise of influencers. We learned as children that people can be popular for no apparent reason whatsoever. This has been reinforced in newer generations via reality television. We've also learned popularity is unstable. You can be exiled as quickly as you are crowned.

Gaining popularity without merit can feel isolating and depressing, even for the person achieving it. Following that path intensely as a viewer and comparing ourselves to the curated version of an influencer's life that is presented as perfect can leave us feeling empty. Feeding on vacant validation makes us hungry and dissatisfied. It's a vicious and codependent cycle. Influence is a powerful tool. Putting it in the right hands at the right time with the right content can be innovative. Conversely, the stakes are high when the influence is being yielded in the opposite direction.

To clarify: I do not put the *expert* or *creator* in the same bucket as the influencer. Creators and experts are a vital part of the digital environment. People who are truly gifted and have worked hard to become experts in a field have found an outlet to express themselves, connect with others, collaborate, and, yes, make money. How wonderful!

It has been heartening to see brands connect with creators and experts they might have not had exposure to otherwise. Not only did social media change the game for customer service, making brands accountable in a public forum, it also allowed brands to see their products being used in fun and visionary ways. They didn't have to think too hard to find inspired ideas anymore—the creators were already doing that.

Identifying and amplifying experts and creators who have influence is the ultimate goal. However, too many brands and their correlating agencies try to take shortcuts and default to the lowest common denominator of getting their product into the hands of people who have amassed popularity. It can make for a perceived quick win for those who don't care about the healthy longevity of the brand or medium. But this can also backfire. If the influencer hired to promote the brand tarnishes their reputation, they can take the brand down along with them. This jeopardizes the viability for a lot of creators out there.

As a long-term contributor to the digital marketing industry, I feel strongly that those of us in the business need to remember what a gift the internet is and how much it adds to our ability to connect to one another worldwide. If we view the internet as a global community, then all of us who interact with it should strive to do so in ways that allow us to feel proud of ourselves.

One of our roles is to be proponents of common sense and moderation in marketing. Those of us in the business should act as advocates, not only for our clients but also for fans and audiences. That said, end users must also accept responsibility when they engage online. We tag our media with our locations and let children whose brains aren't developed enough to understand the consequence of a digital footprint have their own channels while barely monitoring them.

Many parents don't monitor their children's accounts because they don't understand the platform, yet they agree to their children having a profile. There must be some personal responsibility and common sense applied to our usage and restraint, especially for our children.

Scams on fans (or followers) is an old business. If you have ever been hacked or impersonated or bullied online, you know the toll it can take on your time and your emotions. Now imagine that you have thirty clients, each on at least five platforms, and on each of those mediums they are being hacked, impersonated, or bullied daily. That is the reality for digital marketing companies, including Girlilla Marketing.

The blue check marks of social-network verification were highly coveted and often hard to come by. The standards by which your account could be verified were vague at best. Additionally, some platforms allowed users to pay for verification, which, ironically, cheapened its authenticity. As an agency, we have access to portals and tools (and personal contacts at the platforms), but the consistency and transparency is not there for the everyday person to follow.

The system is very flawed. There is no process to prove who you are when you sign up, minus an email, and in some cases, identification for veri-fication. People can create a profile saying they are anyone, and if that happens to be someone famous, the famous person must fight for their name. We spend hours playing what amounts to Whac-A-Mole, searching for our clients' names and content and reporting violations to the platforms.

By simply saying "fan account" somewhere in the bio, many profiles are allowed to stay in operation using a name, likeness, and content that they do not own. Most of these accounts swindle people out of money or, worse, safety. In many cases, by the time we get to them the damage has been done. Fans are becoming savvy to the scams, but the scams are also becoming savvy to the fans.

Personally, I had hoped to see more rules and enforcement from Big Tech even before the 2020 political problems and press coverage. Clear guidelines and consistent enforcement are not too much to ask. If individual public profiles were treated as broadcasters and vetted before going live, and if they adhered to a set of standards similar to those for television and radio, we could not only cut down on imposters and scams but also drastically reduce fake news and false advertisements. It breaks my heart to see respected news outlets using clickbait and trend-jacking to increase site traffic. However, if you make it past the headline and click the media, the outlet needs to be responsible for their work.

We can and should demand safety nets for public profiles and creators (broadcasters) to ensure they are responsible for what they post or share (broadcast). We should all agree that before you post or share as a verified profile, you must confirm what you are sharing is true and verified.

The decade from 2010–2020 saw so much social media growth and impact that it gives me heartburn. After Facebook's initial public offering was the third biggest in US history and the biggest ever for a tech company in the US, many who hadn't paid attention to digital media or dismissed it were suddenly very interested in our strategy. While we were busy with our previous digital duties, we also had to manage strategies on the other networks and messaging apps like Pinterest and LinkedIn. We saw advertising integration and new territories that we hadn't previously had exposure or access to, like Asia. Every year, more opportunities opened up and we became responsible for more duties. I loved the fast pace of it.

The advent of social media put musicians' relationships with their fans on public display. It also profoundly changed the dynamic between them. In the past, artists were primarily limited to scripted, formal interviews. But on social media, artists could tell a story or share an experience in an off-the-cuff, more casual manner. They could reveal a lot more about their personal lives and their creative processes, which forged a deeper connection with their fan bases.

In turn, fans gained a new ability to respond. In addition to feedback from people telling us what they did or didn't like, or if they'd had a great or a bad experience, they also created more robust expressions including performing cover songs, creative collaborations, paintings, photographs, and animated videos.

The digital community has created some other positive elements too. Once I became a mother, this mattered even more as I started thinking about the huge impact technology would have on my children's lives. The digital community is a collection of people engaging with one another. It is responsible for spreading the word on charities or movements that otherwise might not have an outlet. Some social platforms have made it turnkey to raise funds or awareness for causes and organizations. I am extremely pleased that the barrier of entry to do good has been lowered and power has been put into the hands of the people so we can all be involved. I was particularly encouraged when even with 2020's volatile political environment, the COVID-19 pandemic, and general dis-ease of the digital community, we found a way to give even when it felt like we didn't have any more to give.

The longer I work in digital marketing, the more passionate I feel about it. I am contributing positively to a future I want to help create. I had come a long way from my days working at the tanning salon and coffee shop. I was proud of my progress and eager to see what lay in store for me next.

After my daughter was born in 2012, I felt more dedicated than ever to the business. I took eight weeks of maternity leave but felt eager to return to the office afterward. While the transition back was tough, especially because I was still traveling a lot, I made some changes that helped me feel better equipped as a working parent. They included working less at the office and more from home and taking my daughter, who thankfully was an easy baby, along in the BabyBjörn on work outings and trips.

My husband recognizes how important my work is to me. We don't argue or fight over whose career matters more. Instead, we're committed to supporting each other in all areas of our lives, and we co-parent. This even partnership really works for us and our family. I'm grateful that we share values that allow both of us to feel fulfilled at home and at work. Our marriage continues to demonstrate the power of genuine and authentic partnership, something that mattered even more to me when my work partnership with ROAR started to sour.

CHAPTER FIFTEEN

ROAR No More

· 2016-2018 ·

MY BUSINESS PARTNERSHIP accomplished what I'd hoped it would in the first few years—it gave us resources and cushion. I worked happily with the ROAR team when they pitched potential new clients, since those clients might also become Girlilla Marketing accounts too. I needed practice pitching, and the team got me into rooms I was not yet able to get into on my own.

It also made sense to contribute for goodwill when my partners needed help. They surely did help me, especially when I needed guidance on legal, HR, or business-management issues. And they were great sounding boards about ideas. More than partners, I felt like I had friends who were looking out for me.

In the beginning of our union, Girlilla Marketing was new, and no one knew what the business would yield. As time passed and our model became more predictable, we were better able to quantify our value. We soon learned that our biggest asset was our time, which needed to be protected.

We started to track the time we spent on each project. This was a game changer for us. It allowed me to better understand, on average, what to expect per each employee, and eventually what to expect from different levels of employees. We saw how much of our time went into all areas of our business, including proposals, reporting, creating assets, and billing. We learned how to effectively price out future projects and remain profitable on passion projects we wanted to take (even if they came with a smaller budget).

Being treated as part of the whole team was a good thing in many ways. I and the Girlilla Marketing employees were always invited to company functions. We celebrated ROAR's wins with them and felt their pain when they had losses.

One of the fundamental conditions of the acquisition was autonomy. Until the last couple of years of our partnership, most of the time they respected my boundaries. But midway through our arrangement the lines began to blur until it was impossible to ignore.

Instead of being asked to do something or if we wanted to contribute, I felt pressured to prioritize the work my parent company needed over Girlilla Marketing's client work. We started to look and feel more like an interior department of their company. Balancing that delicate equilibrium—on top of being a new mom—forced me to refocus on what I wanted to build and on my professional legacy. I needed to ensure that Girlilla Marketing and my key employees came first.

One project we had been involved with for years became such a time suck for me and my team and was so unfulfilling on every level that I'd been trying to resign from it for over a year. My partners repeatedly talked me into ignoring my gut instincts. I stayed active on the account so as not to rock the boat, even though it was costing us on the Girlilla Marketing bottom line.

I was in pajamas in bed, on maternity leave after the birth of my son in 2016 and still managing challenging postpartum hormones along with a newborn and my daughter, who was only four, when I got a call from my partners.

"Jennie, hey, hold on a minute, I'm gonna get Bernie," Matt said after I picked up the phone.

Once Bernie was on the line, Matt repeated, "Hold on… I'm gonna get Will…"

I straightened up in bed, my heart pounding as I prepared for what I believed was coming: news of some catastrophic disaster.

By this time, the ROAR partners were at odds, litigating heavily among themselves. Bitter rivalries were being waged, and they hated one another. Only a disaster warranted them all getting on a phone call with me. Surely someone had died. A client must have gone off a cliff or gotten into a bus crash. I racked my brain, trying to recall what artists were on tour, but in the month that I'd been on maternity leave details like clients' schedules had blurred.

"Jennie, it's the band." Bernie sounded tentative, as if he were trying to break harsh news softly. This was the client who had thanked Girlilla Marketing when they accepted their Grammy at the awards ceremony. While working with them had stopped being fun and I'd been asking to quit the account for a long while, I hated to think of something bad happening to them. I held my breath, steeling myself against whatever tragedy Bernie was about to share.

"They uh… well… the thing is… they're letting you go." Bernie paused for the briefest of moments, then rushed on. "It's nothing you've done. They just want to try something new."

I let out a huge sigh of relief. This was far less dramatic than the scenarios I had imagined. Of course I was drastically disappointed but ultimately not surprised at being fired while I was on maternity leave. It said a lot about the partners that they were willing to put aside their personal differences to reach out to me collectively. I appreciated their support and respected them, unlike the client.

I hung up the phone and took stock of the situation. It would have felt much more dignified had I been able to resign. Girlilla Marketing hadn't done anything wrong. We didn't fail in any way. The client just didn't value us anymore. Maybe they never truly did.

This negative experience was a big lesson for me. It really hurt, and I needed to feel that to understand how I didn't want to feel ever again. I took it very personally. I was angry that I hadn't been allowed to quit when I wanted to. There were lessons to be learned for how to handle my business in the future. The project had set Girlilla Marketing up for many successes. We were able to get in a lot of doors because of the work we had done for the client. I felt determined to turn this into something I could use.

The first thing I needed to do was forgive. It was hard. I didn't want to. I wanted to be bitter and angry. But in my heart, I knew that what I was feeling in that moment wasn't permanent or productive. I wanted to walk confidently back into my office after my maternity leave knowing that I had recaptured my power. I knew from the nature of our business that we weren't entitled to long-term commitments. But I had attached our identity to the project, and it was my ego that was troubling me. I could certainly remedy that.

On my first day back from maternity leave I sent the client a text thanking them for allowing us to be part of their journey. I also gave a big thank-you to the Universe for the lessons I knew I'd carry with me from the experience.

* * *

When I first joined forces with my partners, our plan was to grow Girlilla Marketing into a thriving, successful business and then sell it. Around the time we hit the five-year mark, several large media companies inquired about possible acquisition. But as we explored the options together, the idea of working underneath other umbrellas wasn't exciting to me.

The prospect of selling raised a lot of questions. Was I equipped to be an employee again? Weren't my biggest struggles over autonomy and control? Besides money, what was the upside of selling? Would my key employees have more security? Better benefits? A path to retirement?

After unsuccessfully expanding our offices and dealing with the ebb and flow of an inflating and deflating client roster over the years, the idea of taking our small shop and drastically expanding felt lackluster to me. I hadn't fully stretched my wings on what I wanted to do with Girlilla Marketing on my own. And the last thing I wanted was to be the kind of CEO who dealt only in Human Resources or Finance.

I wanted the company to be "boutique" by choice. I wanted to be choosy, to remain fully engaged in marketing, and to know all my employees and clients well. I *was* Girlilla Marketing, and I wasn't done. So I doubled down on what I knew the business could be.

Initially, I didn't want to split from my partners. Although it became obvious there was no benefit to either side in keeping the relationship as it was, there wasn't anything urgent about changing the arrangement… until we started fighting and resenting each other.

With selling Girlilla Marketing off the table (which would have been ROAR's biggest payoff for investing in us those first few years), there wasn't a shiny trophy at the end of the road for them either. Tensions were running high in their company. What we'd had in the beginning—a fun, mutually respectful and beneficial relationship—turned into a political shitstorm I had to operate within as the partners argued among themselves. It was impossible to please one partner without alienating another. The dynamic felt far too familiar to a child of divorced parents. I knew how to dance the dance, but Girlilla Marketing was running at full capacity, and I had two young children. I had little tolerance for acrimonious meetings and wasted time. Our books were balanced, and I knew our value. Besides feeling obligated to try to work things out (and we did try… several times over), I couldn't put my finger on a good reason to stay.

The last few weeks of our partnership were stressful and upsetting. We collectively pursued several different angles, all culminating in dead ends and hurt feelings. While I had doubts about ripping the safety net out from underneath Girlilla Marketing, I also had nearly a decade of experience to know that *security* is a marketing term. No one was better suited to look after the company than I. You can lose yourself in any relationship. I had lost myself and what was best for Girlilla Marketing trying to be a good business partner.

I flew to Los Angeles for one last sit-down with the partners, hoping to come to an understanding. We met in a restaurant. Dinner quickly devolved into a pissing match among them. After months of trying to reach an agreement about my value as a partner in their business, I was tired of being a pawn in their infighting.

Soon after we ordered our meal, it was clear that the meeting wasn't going to end any better than our previous attempts at resolution. I grew so frustrated that before dinner was over I lost my temper and stormed out of the restaurant. I immediately directed my attorneys to dissolve the partnership even if that meant giving up the company name, Girlilla Marketing.

In hindsight, I would have done one hundred things differently. I regretted letting the situation reach the point where frustration and anger got the better of me. I hated that I had put my precious brand, which was so closely attached to me personally, in jeopardy. While the partners bore the brunt of my tantrum, I was angrier at myself for not pro-actively acting on my intuition much earlier.

The conversations that came next were hard. I stopped asking for resolution and started demanding it. I had to get my ducks in a row on the legal side, which is always hard for me, as I have a strong distaste for over-lawyering. This was the most intim-idating part of the separation process, since three of the ROAR partners were attorneys.

My awesome husband, always the voice of reason, gave me his full support to move ahead no matter the outcome. I spent many hours on the phone with my former boss Jay Frank, who coached me endlessly and patiently, and with several Nashville business mentors who were generous with their time and confidentiality.

My legal team advised that it would be easier to walk away from my brand and start anew. I fired them before we finalized any plans. If they weren't willing to fight with me, I wasn't with the right team. I was prepared to start over if I had to, but to not even try to come to some sort of understanding didn't add up to me. I spent hours on the phone with each of the partners, pleading with them to let me have my brand. This was a very complicated ask, as they were still in the middle of their own litigation among themselves, and Girlilla Marketing was an entangled asset.

In the end, one partner held out. I had to call and beg for my company name.

"Please let me go," I urged, making no effort to hide my desperation. "I have a family. I have twelve employees, and they're all going to come with me whether the company is called Girlilla Marketing or something else. Our clients are all coming with us too. I'm prepared to start over, but that name is *me*."

The partner vaguely said he'd think about it but he couldn't make me any promises, and we hung up. I stood for a moment with the phone in my hand, thinking through my next steps.

Giving his colleagues the proverbial middle finger by refusing to let me go and making me collateral damage in the war among the ROAR partners must have lost its luster. Despite their own knotty situation, the partners finally agreed to let me purchase my company name back from them.

CHAPTER SIXTEEN

ReBOOT

· 2017–2018 ·

ONCE WE SPLIT off from ROAR, the pressure to succeed seemed insurmountable. I had more than livelihoods on the line; I had lives. When I founded Girlilla Marketing, Ashley, Stevie, and I were bright-eyed, mostly single, and didn't have kids. We'd seen each other through lean and uncertain years, first houses, marriages, and motherhood. We'd endured turmoil, sickness, grief, and what seemed like a new business plan every single year. We shared many celebrations and subsequent hangovers.

Now I had to explain to Ashley and Stevie that we were soon going to be back on our own but that I couldn't share the details yet. I had to ask them to blindly trust me. These women, who had trusted me with nearly a decade of their professional lives, jumped off a cliff with me. Only now we were no longer young single ladies having fun in the entertainment business. We were wives, homeowners, and mothers, and we'd spent the past decade bleeding everything we had into our jobs. Although I am sure they were scared and anxious, they didn't blink.

On October 1, 2017, with a wiped-out bank account but the Girlilla Marketing name solely under my control once more, and with the support of my team and loyal clients, we opened for business... again. I expected to feel like the bottom had dropped out from underneath me. Instead, I felt brighter. The hardest part of the process was the final decision to split from my partnership. Everything transitioned respectfully and we retained a couple of their clients. I felt grateful for the experiences with them. It taught me what I wanted and made what I didn't want undeniably clear.

In the beginning of the split, anger ran high on both sides. I was close to the extended ROAR team, and especially Bernie, who was like a brother to me. The breakup felt more traumatic than my divorce. Bernie and I didn't speak for a long time. Eventually, though, work brought us back together. Even though our personal relationship was in disrepair, we provided better results for our clients when we worked as a team. Over the years, our friendship has been repaired and evolved.

The top of Girlilla Marketing's first year after I bought the company back was extremely busy. Technically, we were celebrating our ten-year anniversary. It felt good to hit that milestone. Pete's question came to mind again. It had touched off my journey into becoming an entrepreneur. I was proud of myself for following through on my dreams and felt okay taking a minute to savor that. We made a couple of bold moves, like acquiring another firm, reconfiguring our services, and cleaning house on anything I no longer wanted to be a part of.

We had immense support from the business and press communities. Everyone and everything I needed came from the connections and friends I had made in Nashville. When I was feeling down, insecure, or tired, I had people to rely on. Between my husband, mentors, friends, and my core team, I was happier than I had felt in a long time.

After buying my company back, I was operating close to the line. My grandmother used to say that if you didn't have the cash to buy the TV, you didn't buy the TV. We functioned with what we had and with a line of credit from Pinnacle Bank. I am proud to say that we went on to have the healthiest financial year to that point in our history.

Being an independent organization again allowed me to be more present in the community. I was still heeding what I considered some of the best business advice I'd ever gotten and doing my best to help people, as Nikki had said. Over the years, I've felt honored to sit on charitable boards such as St. Jude, the Country Music Association Foundation, and Music Health Alliance. What I have received back in terms of friendship and mentorship far outweighs the commitment to serve. People including Joe Galante, Sarah Trahern, Tiffany Kerns, Tatum Hauck Allsep, and Jackie Proffit have helped me grow in my positions, be a better friend, and use my skill sets to give back. Most importantly, all of them offered big, strong shoulders to cry on when I needed help the most.

As 2018 came to an end, I found myself leaning on everyone in my circle of friends and community when an unexpected diagnosis threatened not just my career but my life.

CHAPTER SEVENTEEN

ONe iN EiGHT

· 2018–2019 ·

IT'S KIND OF AMAZING how the Universe works. I was on the phone with a friend/client, Haley McLemore, who mentioned that she'd just had a mammogram and had gotten called back for an ultrasound. Worried, I asked if that was normal. Haley explained that it was, especially if you have big, dense boobs. We laughed about it, as we laugh about most things together.

Talking to Haley turned into a huge blessing. That conversation triggered me to schedule a mammogram—only my second, as I was just forty-one years old. Had Haley not mentioned her mammogram, I might have put off scheduling mine until Vanderbilt University Medical Center reminded me.

My first mammogram a year earlier had been normal. No one in my immediate family had breast cancer. I knew the importance of testing, and after Pete's illness I took cancer seriously, but there was no reason to think I was at risk. My son was just two at the time, so I wasn't far out of baby mode. I saw my doctors regularly for postpartum care and was aware of my body and its changes after breastfeeding.

Vanderbilt was able to squeeze me in later that week (pun intended). I got the call to return for an ultrasound the next day. Recalling my conversation with Haley, I didn't think anything of it other than feeling inconvenienced because they wanted me back quickly and I had to rearrange my schedule.

After the ultrasound, my doctor wanted to do a biopsy. I knew from experience that biopsies are a little painful, a lot uncomfortable, and stressful. (My dentist discovered some lumps in my neck in 2012.

One in Eight

That biopsy revealed several benign masses attached to my thyroid. I had surgery to remove half of the gland.)

When I hung up the phone after scheduling the breast biopsy, the what-ifs started popping in my brain. Thinking of Haley, I told myself the additional tests were a routine precaution, pushed aside the negative thoughts, and went back to my to-do list.

I told Shannon and a few people close to me that I needed to have a biopsy, but I was so calm about the procedure that I went by myself. Afterward, as I changed back into my clothes, I read one of the pink signs plastered in every hallway and room. It explained that one in eight women receives a positive breast cancer diagnosis. As I exited the waiting room, I counted all the women there and averaged the number of patients the imaging center sees in a day, a week, a month, a year. I still didn't think I would be the one in eight.

The next night, November 8, 2018, Shannon was in Los Angeles on business. When I got home from work, I juggled making dinner and answering evening emails. Then I put my son into bed. While my daughter went to her room to put her pajamas on, I took a bath.

My phone rang as I was toweling off. I squinted at the screen through beads of water dripping in front of my eyes, recognized the Vanderbilt University Medical Center number, and punched the Answer button.

"Jennie?" My primary-care physician's voice filled my ear. She wasted no time on niceties. "The results of your biopsy came back. I'm afraid that you have cancer."

In one instant, my entire life changed. I didn't collapse in a heap or become hysterical. I withdrew somewhere deep inside and watched myself from a distance instead of fully experiencing what was happening. I heard myself ask the doctor if I was going to die. She skirted the blunt question and kindly told me she would call the next day to go over details after she spoke with the oncologist.

I hung up in a daze. The rest of the night felt surreal. I was still soaking wet, my skin red from the bath, when I slipped my robe on. I wondered if my cancer was somehow connected to Pete's and how my diagnosis would affect my daughter, my sister, and my niece.

I moved down the hallway on autopilot to turn on the night-lights and music in my daughter's room. "Hey, sweetie, I want you to have good dreams, okay?" My voice rang with false cheer as I climbed her bunk-bed steps and kissed her sweet head. *She's so little. How is she going to live without her mom?* I wondered. My vision blurred again, this time from tears.

"Mommy, what's wrong?" My daughter frowned and pursed her lips. She sensed something was up, so I hurried the bedtime routine along, forcing myself to hold back the emotion building in me until I was out of her room.

I hurried back downstairs, shaking and sobbing. My mind raced as I moved into the kitchen. I tried to soothe my growing panic by distracting myself with loading the dishwasher. A flood of questions filled my mind. *How was I going to work? What would happen to my dogs? Would it hurt to lose my hair? Who would tell my little boy I loved him? Would he remember me if I didn't make it?*

It's silly, the things you think about when your mortality is suddenly at stake. I remember feeling mad that I hadn't taken out more life insurance. I couldn't believe this was happening to me. Surely it was an error. A nightmare to be woken up from.

My voice shook when I called Shannon. I have no idea what I said to him, other than that he needed to catch the red-eye home. He raced to LAX to catch a flight.

I didn't sleep that night while I waited for him to make his way back across the country. I made a few short phone calls to my sister, my closest friends, and Ashley, my right-hand person at the office. I don't remember anything I said. I felt like I was leaving a trail of shock behind me, as I had zero information beyond what the doctor had told me.

Images of Pete, shrunken and emaciated during his last days, rose in my mind like gruesome Whac-A-Moles. No matter how many times I shoved them down they rose again, ferocious and insistent. Alone and raw in those dark, quiet hours while I waited for the dawn to bring my husband home, I acknowledged that I had to prepare for the fight of my life.

I recalled the night in Pete's apartment when I'd wanted so badly to take the meds in his medicine cabinet to make my pain disappear. Instead, I'd turned to God for help. So much more was hanging in the balance now, with Shannon, the kids, and my business. Surely this was a huge mistake. I had already been through enough. What did I do to get cancer?

My next thought was, *Why* not *me?* Somehow, through my shock and anger I realized that I knew better than to succumb to self-pity and despair. Being mad at God wasn't going to help. I needed my faith now more than ever.

Over the next few days, I wasn't sure exactly what kind of cancer I had, or how we were going to fight it, so it was hard to identify with or receive comfort from anyone. I tried to stay off the internet, but it was impossible not to look. I reveled in the stories of survivors, grateful for celebrities who shared their stories.

At first, I tried to keep things light around the kids. I tried to share honestly but stick only to what they needed to know in a way they could understand. I couldn't look my twenty-year-old stepdaughter, Cassidy, in the eyes for fear I'd break down sobbing as I shared the news. I didn't want her to worry, but I also wanted her to be prepared.

When I told Holly Harrell, our so-much-more-than-a nanny, I thought, *Will she be able to shoulder the burden of caring for the kids emotionally as well as physically through this?* Holly is very special to our family. She had lost her mother at a young age, and I was afraid that my diagnosis might trigger anxiety for her too. Incredibly, Holly was able to look beyond her own losses and support me throughout my treatment and recovery. Today I get a huge thrill out of watching her as a mom to her own son.

Many well-intentioned friends called and texted to check in on me. While I deeply appreciated their concern, they were also looking for answers I didn't have. Soon I regretted telling anyone. I panicked whenever I got a text asking, "How are you? Any news?" Women in their early forties don't get cancer often, and it's normal for people to ask questions. I struggled between feeling lucky that I had friends who cared enough to ask me how I was doing and feeling stressed out about the comfort that people were waiting for me to give them about my situation.

I didn't want to avoid my friends and colleagues who were concerned about me. I also didn't want to repeat myself over and over. And I needed space to absorb the news myself. I also needed to feel a sense of normalcy. In rare moments when I was able to focus on something besides the diagnosis and play with my kids or work or eat pizza, a well-intentioned call or text sent me right back into a maelstrom of anxiety.

Eventually I turned to what I always do when I need to sort things out in my head: I wrote. I sent a blind carbon copy email to my loved ones explaining what was happening and how I was feeling. This gave me an opportunity to make sure I had the details right and work through my feelings. It also allowed me to share without taking more time away from my family or my work, as keeping energy up for either of those became a great feat.

In some ways having breast cancer is a lot like being pregnant. You get unsolicited advice and cautionary tales of doom and gloom. People mean well and want to connect, but these kinds of shares rarely offer soothing, comfort, or encouragement. No one says, "Yeah, my birth was pretty normal. Everything was fine." Instead, you get "My mom labored for seventy-two hours and then had a C-section" or "My cousin hasn't been right since that episiotomy" or "You aren't going to get an epidural, are you?"

I had a hard time when people heard about my disease and said things like, "My grandmother passed away from breast cancer" or "Have you researched alternative treatments? I read this article…" or "I hear a lot of women die from that." Here's my all-time favorite: "Essential oils really helped my sister's friend."

There's also a misconception that getting "new boobs" is a perk of breast cancer. I sometimes fell back on that comedy routine too. If people were going to talk about my boobs, I wanted to control the narrative, and I usually did so with humor or sarcasm.

I don't remember celebrating Thanksgiving that year, or any of our traditional preparation for the Christmas holiday. Instead of enjoying the festive season, I was thrust into a system and schedule I eventually managed like another full-time job. I went to Vanderbilt Medical Center almost every day for MRIs, genetic testing, and lab work. I vacillated between operating on emotional autopilot and sobbing uncontrollably.

At work, Ashley and Stevie took everything they could off my plate. There were things that only I could do, and that was okay. I relished any moments when I felt like my old self, even for just a few seconds.

In mid-December, a month after my diagnosis, I underwent a lumpectomy in my right breast and had lymph nodes removed. Dr. R. Daniel Beauchamp, my surgical oncologist, was wonderful. His calm, confident demeanor soothed me. I trusted him, and that helped me feel a lot better.

The initial tissue tests identified my cancer as HER2+, which tends to be more aggressive than some other types of breast cancer but also receptive to treatment. The good news was they didn't see cancer in my nodes, which meant spreading was unlikely. The bad news was that the margins (the perimeters around the removed cancer) weren't clear. I'd have to have another lumpectomy after the holidays. I would also have to undergo nine immunotherapy infusions of Herceptin, twelve rounds of Taxol chemotherapy, and radiation. Then I'd probably take tamoxifen for the next ten years. After learning I'd be undergoing treatment for most of 2019, I spent the Christmas season in a haze. I distinctly remember feeling numb and rattling off the plan to friends.

A strange thing happened after I learned that I had cancer. I built up a tolerance to bad news. I learned that while I might be disappointed by a diagnosis or complication with treatment, I couldn't allow myself to grow hopeless. Somehow, I just kept going.

I was surprised by those who supported me in a meaningful way, as well as by those who didn't, or couldn't. At times I felt jealous of healthy people who took their health for granted, and mad at people who complained about things that don't matter. I also realized that at various times I have been the good friend, the bad friend, the pushy friend, the absent friend, the person who has taken her healthy body for granted. Now I was the person realizing that people just don't know how to act or what to say. I decided to forgive them and love them anyway.

Connecting with others who understood what I was going through was crucial to my recovery. My former boss and mentor Jay Frank was suffering from a more aggressive form of cancer. For decades Jay had been like an older brother. I looked to him for examples of how to succeed not just in business but in relationships and parenting. I trusted his insightful wisdom. Now he jumped in and gave me the pointers that only a cancer patient could give. He told me what questions to ask, treatment decisions not to back down on, and the real scoop on how to tackle my treatment. Jay knew that if I had the information I needed, I'd process it and get busy healing.

Phran Galante, another friend in the throes of her own intense cancer battle, swooped in and took me under her wing. She always seemed to know when I was breaking down and called to lift my spirits. Jay and Phran both checked in with me after every surgery and round of chemotherapy. Sometimes Jay and I had chemo on the same day. We kept each other company over the phone from our respective waiting rooms. Jay's case was much more advanced than mine, but his concern for me never wavered.

Phran was in pain, but you wouldn't know it by her selflessness or her high heels. Her love and understanding carried me through dark moments. Had I known how many of those were awaiting me in the year ahead, I might not have had the strength to face them alone. Luckily, I didn't have to.

My cancer confidant circle that started with Jay and Phran expanded. While I knew that there were organizations and support groups for cancer patients and their families, sitting in a room with strangers was not for me. A text, phone call, or coffee meeting where I could say what I felt without any judgment meant everything.

Lisa Lee, a dear friend I had worked with for years, was fighting a brain tumor. Being part of her journey motivated me on my healing path too.

Stevie Frasure, a fellow breast-cancer survivor, sent a comprehensive and hilarious mastectomy letter and a basketful of practical things to use during my recovery. I have passed her words of wisdom on to several women on their own breast cancer journeys.

I try to be a good steward, especially of the examples that Jay, Phran, and Lisa set for me. I miss them, but when I get to help someone else, I feel like I am honoring their legacies and keeping their lessons alive. I hope I have the honor to continue to help anyone who needs me.

CHAPTER EIGHTEEN

Hairy Times

· 2019 ·

MID-JANUARY 2019, I rolled up for the first of nine Herceptin immunotherapy infusions at Vanderbilt. When I walked through the infusion clinic doors, I was immediately transported to another world, one in which nurses and other health-care providers administered the clinical components of physical healing with compassion, comfort, and warmth. Their smiles and kind eyes reassured me they knew where I was going and they would accompany me all the way. Every single caregiver in the clinic had my back. One of the first nurses I met was a cancer survivor. Another was from my home state. Tiffani, who I talked *Game of Thrones* with, became my friend. Another nurse mailed me a copy of *Jesus Calling* that I still read every day.

The immunotherapy sessions were like dress rehearsal for chemotherapy. I mastered the process of parking, waiting, labs, waiting, setting up, waiting, finally getting the drugs in the pipe, and then waiting some more. I heard patients ring the bell when they completed treatment or received a clean bill of health. I heard others cry. I watched feet shuffle past my area beneath the pulled curtain around my space, and I saw people I somehow knew weren't going to make it.

The nurses worked briskly and efficiently, like they had a mundane job. Sometimes while I sat in my chair surrounded by people who were even sicker than I was, I caught snatches of conversations between the clinic employees about lunch or weekend plans or, better yet, some workplace bitchiness. While I would have given anything to be back at Girlilla Marketing dealing with my own workplace shenanigans, the drama in the clinic transported me, even just for a few minutes, to a world that seemed a little more normal than my own was now. I looked forward to those moments and drew comfort from them in the year that followed.

* * *

On January 21, 2019, I had my second lumpectomy. I remember seeing Dr. Beauchamp just before the surgery. The mood was rather jovial. While the margins weren't clean after the initial procedure, I was feeling stronger, and Dr. Beauchamp was confident that this time the margins would get cleared and I'd soon be ready for chemo and radiation.

The procedure seemed quick this time. I got out of recovery and was home and back to work a lot faster than the first time, which relieved me. I vastly preferred to focus on my clients rather than on my treatment.

When the results came back, the margins still weren't clear. We had to change the treatment plan again and either do a third lumpectomy or move forward with chemotherapy. By then, I was tired of fucking around. It was already February, three months after my diagnosis. True to my spirited nature, I wanted to get the show on the road. While breast cancer is slower-moving than other types of cancers, knowing it was still in my body made me very uneasy.

After consulting with my oncologist and Dr. Beauchamp, I opted to start chemotherapy. I also decided to have a double mastectomy after chemo. I chose this option for a few reasons. A third lumpectomy meant I'd need reconstructive surgery, something I hoped to avoid. A double mastectomy offered the best odds of avoiding recurrence in my case, and it meant I didn't need to have radiation.

I'd like to say I was the type of girl who would say "fuck it" and shave her head before chemo. I wasn't. After my failed lumpectomies and knowing the doctors would soon remove my breasts and pump me full of hormones, I concentrated intently on finding a way to salvage something of myself.

When I found out about cold-cap therapy, I lit up with hope. This modality has helped many people keep some of their hair during treatment. Cold caps are tightly fitting, helmetlike hats filled with a freezing-cold gel or liquid worn for hours before, during, and after chemotherapy infusions. A long list of processes must be consistently and meticulously followed pre- and post-chemo.

My friend Jamie introduced me to Lacey Steih, who works with Penguin Cold Caps. During our first conversation she didn't just share facts about cold-cap therapy, she also comforted me and offered advice. Lacey had sat for hours with cancer patients at several different facilities. She warned me that cold-cap therapy isn't for the faint of heart. It is expensive and calls for a high pain tolerance. To date, very few facilities offer this service. Even fewer insurance companies cover it, even though it's common practice in other countries and science has proven its validity.

It felt kind of silly, but losing my hair mattered to me. I wanted one single thing I could control, so I said yes to the cold-cap therapy. While the medical community might not validate this treatment method, I have a full head of hair. I did lose my lashes and brows several times, but they're back now too.

Lacey also tipped me off about icing my hands and feet to help prevent neuropathy. I stopped suffering symptoms when I submerged my hands and feet in ice during chemo treatments. While the Vanderbilt infusion clinic didn't officially endorse cold-cap therapy or ice therapy to lessen neuropathy, there was a big ice machine in the clinic, and that spoke volumes to me.

* * *

My first chemotherapy session took place on February 2, 2019. Between pre-drugs, immunotherapy, chemotherapy, and cold-cap therapy, I clocked a ten-hour day. My nerves were shot. I didn't know how I was going to feel when I got home and in the days after. Suddenly all the anxiety of three months of wondering what chemo treatment was going to be like raced through me. I couldn't make firm plans for work or anything else. Ashley and Stevie assured me I could take all the time I needed, but I was jacked up on adrenaline, uncertainty, and worry.

The room pods were small and could only hold one person in addition to the patient. The nurses accommodated Lacey and her huge cooler of ice caps (which she sat on every week... I can't imagine that was comfortable). My husband worked from the hallway or anywhere he could. He was my rock throughout my treatments.

After that first chemo session, Shannon and I walked to our car in the parking lot. I started to feel nauseous and feared I was going to have diarrhea in the car. I wasn't sure I could last the short ride. It was sad and humiliating, and suddenly very real.

I had been prepped to stay on top of symptoms and had a huge basket of prescriptions and over-the-counter meds ready to take on my nightstand. I got home, locked myself in the bathroom, threw up, and wept. I had been doing a lot better emotionally since the diagnosis, feeling stronger after the lumpectomies and taking care of myself in preparation for chemotherapy. But less than an hour had passed, and I felt awful. I scraped myself off the bathroom floor, crawled into bed, popped some Imodium, and soon felt better. I just had an upset stomach, probably brought on by nerves.

Later chemotherapy treatments were hours shorter than the first since I didn't have immuno-therapy too. After I had two chemo treatments under my belt, I understood the pattern of symptoms. The steroids kept me up the first night and fortified the second day, so I tried to work as much as possible and do things around the house then. During the third and fourth days I battled symptoms including extreme fatigue, nausea, headache, and hypersensitivity. I felt

run-down and like I had the flu. As a working mom
of two, I knew from experience that I could power
through, but I also needed to keep myself strong
to ward off infections. I slept when I could. I ate
well. I set up a workstation in my bedroom (great
training ground for the future COVID pandemic).
My so-much-more-than-a-nanny, Holly, and my
stepdaughter, Cassidy, picked up a lot of slack with
the younger kids.

I missed a lot during the long months of
treatment. I could hear life happening outside my
bedroom door as I lay in bed for long stretches.
Laughter, crying, and even yelling sounded like a
party I ached to join. I felt angry about missing out.
I worried about how long the business could thrive
without me. Then I started to wonder if the business might be *just fine* without me. Neither stream
of thought felt good.

My son was so young that he doesn't remember
seeing me down for the count. The hardest part,
besides being sick and fatigued for the better part of

a year, was being physically unable to pick him up.

Occasionally my daughter tiptoed reluctantly into my room. She was used to my vibrant, energetic nature. The subdued version of me lingering in bed for days scared her. Whenever she gently asked when I was going to feel better, all I could tell her was, "Soon."

My oncology team told me repeatedly that because I was receiving twelve chemotherapy treatments in twelve weeks, I needed to be prepared for cumulative effects. Shannon and I both agreed that, although things were scary, it was better for him to work and travel now and stay home later when I had my double mastectomy and reconstruction surgery. I was happy to see him off at the airport, not only because I wanted him to continue working but because his life had been thrown upside down too. I hoped that for a few days he could maybe forget about my cancer, although he never said a word about needing that.

My sister came to stay while Shannon was gone.

It was so nice having Kelley with me. I felt relieved having my big sis in the next room, knowing that I didn't have to talk and pretend to feel well. I could relax and let her do her thing.

Three days after my third treatment, searing pain shot through my left ear. It started on a weekend. Nothing about it was routine. As instructed, I called the oncology department before I sought care anywhere else. I relayed my symptoms to the doctor on call, who said it was most likely an ear infection.

Then I started to bleed out of my ear and was sent to the emergency room. The ER doctor didn't see an infection. I was told that I might have a ruptured eardrum and sent home, still in excruciating pain. The pressure and drainage in my ear escalated. At some point, I lost hearing in the ear completely (minus hearing the *boom, boom, boom* of my heartbeat). I couldn't stand on my own due to pain and balance issues.

I called oncology again. I still hadn't spoken to my oncologist, only the on-call service. Feeling deflated and ignored, I went back to the emergency room. The same ER doctor apologized profusely and found a room for me, where the infectious disease team took over.

When I didn't respond to medication, they phoned in an IV antibiotic, vancomycin, what the doctor called the "last call" of antibiotics. I was still bleeding and leaking fluid out of my ear (enough to soak through towels) and was in pain, despite the ER doing everything they could with the limited list of pain meds and antibiotics I wasn't allergic to.

I recall one of the infectious disease doctors coming into my room and giving me a big dose of comfort. She told me that her mother was a breast-cancer survivor and that her mom's journey was a large part of why she decided to become a physi-cian. When she shared her experience as a little girl growing up with her mom being sick, I hung on every word, imagining that my daughter must be having a similar experience.

Somewhere in my fuzzy state, feeling in limbo

between the infectious disease team and the oncology team (who we couldn't get ahold of), I remembered my otolaryngologist, Dr. John Seibert, who had operated on my thyroid. I emailed him from my hospital bed and told him what was happening. He got one of his colleagues at the hospital to see me, and I finally felt like someone was trying to help.

Dr. Seibert and his nurse, Susan, became a big part of my care team. He determined that I had mastoiditis, which is rare in adults, and explained why I wasn't responding to the ear-infection or ruptured-eardrum treatments. The infection was severe, and since I was immunocompromised, my health-care team was worried about the infection traveling from the mastoid into my brain. I was so sick I couldn't continue chemotherapy until I was better.

When a bed finally opened on the oncology unit the next day, I was transferred there from the ER. They were still giving me vancomycin to miti-gate the infection. A kind nurse tipped me off that I didn't need to be in the hospital to get the treatment. I could be in my own bed, with home health care. Since it was a holiday weekend and I would most likely not speak to my oncologist until the workweek began, I was extremely grateful for her insights.

With no additional answers and a bag full of balloon drugs, Shannon took me home, where the home health-care team taught me how to flush my own port. I had to administer the vancomycin every few hours. For the first time since surgery and starting chemotherapy, I was relegated to staying home and had to rely on everyone to help me.

When I finally made it to my oncologist's office, I was told, "Most people tolerate this treatment very well," and the mastoiditis was brushed off as probably not cancer related. I tried to address the communication gap over the holiday weekend, but that was dismissed as an administrative error.

As a leader and a boss, I felt disappointed by my medical team's failure to take responsibility. But it was a great lesson. The care that I expected from my oncologist wasn't realistic. I expected a similar level of care to what I had received in surgery. However, it was clear that I should only expect administrative help with plans, appointments, prescriptions, and task-oriented duties. Once I understood that and worked directly with the nurses in the department, my expectations were better managed.

Thanks to Dr. Seibert's care, I improved enough to resume chemo in less than two weeks. I was still in pain and couldn't hear, but I felt relieved to continue with my cancer treatment.

I learned a lot from this experience. The first and most important lesson was that I would no longer take no for an answer when I knew something was wrong and I needed treatment. I wouldn't fear coming off as bitchy or pushy, or degrade myself by feeling bad about advocating for myself. This experience reminded me of how I'd had to stand up for Pete in his last days. It also called to mind how detrimental ignoring my intuition is in all areas of my life.

It was difficult for me to talk on the phone for a couple of months. My body and balance adjusted to not hearing well on the left side, but whenever I put the phone to my right ear, it threw me off. But I never missed a call from Jay or an email from Phran. Anytime I questioned whether I could handle any more challenges in my treatment, I remembered Phran writing to me that this journey is full of surprises. She gently reminded me not to compare myself to other patients or allow any setbacks to get the better of me and my hope for a complete recovery.

I also frequently recalled Jay telling me, "Some people get chemo so they don't die as soon. *You* are getting chemo so you can live."

At my dear mentor's reminder, I resolved to never complain again.

CHAPTER NINETEEN

Brand-New Boobs

· 2019 ·

IN EARLY MAY, after I completed chemotherapy, I met the plastic surgeon who was going to perform my double mastectomy. Stuffed in a small exam room at the Breast Center at Vanderbilt, Dr. Kent "Kye" Higdon said what I had desperately longed to hear: "You know you're going to be okay, right?"

The answer was no, I didn't know that I was going to be okay. When the cancer was originally detected, the radiologist had been quick to reassure me I would be fine. But over the seven months of surgeries and chemotherapy I wasn't given any indication that any of it was working. When Dr. Higdon reassured me, I hugged him and wept.

On June 3, 2019, I saw Dr. Beauchamp and Dr. Higdon for a brief presurgery meeting, then they wheeled me into the operating room. "Eye of the Tiger" was playing over the speakers. I laughed at the fitting musical selection and then drifted off to sleep feeling like I had finally reached a recovery milestone.

For the first time, not only did things go as planned, they went better than expected. They were able to perform a nipple- and skin-sparing procedure, and my expanders looked pretty darn normal underneath clothing. My pain was significant and my mobility extremely limited, but I forced myself to walk as soon as possible. I felt better within days. Sleeping was another level of special hell, but armed with maternity pillows and neck braces from Stevie Frasure's recommendations, I built myself a pillow contraption to keep from rolling over in my sleep.

On June 12—eight months after my

diagnosis—the pathology came back favorable. When I saw Dr. Beauchamp the next day for a follow-up appointment, I cried on him too. Everything over the next several months meant zilch after hearing "We got it." Drains, labs, saline expansions, even my still-troublesome ear paled in comparison to the relief and exhilaration I felt. I was beginning to feel hopeful again and cautiously optimistic that I could regain the rich, full life I had worked so hard to create.

The days between the mastectomy and reconstruction were still full of treatments, labs, and appointments, but I was able to resume more of my life, including being more involved in the business again.

We lost Phran a few days before my reconstruction surgery in September 2019, and we lost Jay soon after. I was devastated. I was unable to see either one of them to say goodbye because I was immuno- compromised. Their loved ones read them the letters I wrote to each of them, which I feel so grateful for.

I wrote to Phran,

There is no one on earth who I would drink Fireball for… except you. In fact, I'd probably do anything you told me to do because (a) I am fairly certain you could take me in a street fight, and (b) I knew from the moment we took a stroll around the block in New York City that you were the kind of woman who, given a chance to come in contact with, you hold on to.

I also told her,

When I heard from you after I got cancer… you gave me real talk, real focus. There were no fragile-cupcake conversations, just a whole lot of understanding, encouragement, and inappropriateness that induced much-needed laughter. Every time you reached out it was always perfect timing. You knew exactly what to say at the exact time I needed to hear it.

To Jay I wrote,

When I think about my big life-changing moments—career, moving, friendship/mentorship, parenting, cancer—you are a constant. Twenty years ago, when you took a chance on me, you changed my life. I was unruly and underqualified and unmanageable. But somehow you did it. You taught me by making me better in all the areas I wasn't (you made me admit what those were first) and celebrated with me when I became better and more confident. You gave me a seat at the table and made me feel that I was just taking the seat that had my name on it. That's more than any teacher or parent did for me in my whole life... and it carried over into so many more areas than work.

I am so grateful to Phran and Jay. I feel confident that they both knew how much I loved them. I carry their lessons with me as part of their incredible legacies.

* * *

As promised, Dr. Higdon got me in and out of the reconstruction surgery with no major problems (and a few laughs). This last surgery was a big line item to check off my list, and I do so love to finish a to-do list.

Dr. Beauchamp retired soon after my last surgery. Unbeknownst to me, while he was treating me, he was fighting his own illness too. He lost his battle in 2022. I am just one person among thousands he helped. I think of him often and will be grateful for him forever.

October is Breast Cancer Awareness Month. In 2019, it was a month shy of a year from my diagnosis. My friend and publicist, Jacquelyn Marushka, posted on Instagram from a waiting room about getting her mammogram. One woman commented that she had cancelled her appointment over concerns of radiation exposure and false test results. I felt dumbfounded as well as inspired to start advocating for screenings and early detection. I was a little shy about putting myself out there, but if my story could incite someone to schedule their mammogram appointment, I was all in.

Jacquelyn connected me with a beautiful writer and kind soul, Tricia Despres, who helped me articulate my cancer journey for an online article on People.com. This was the first time that I looked back over the past year through the lens of a hopeful future. Women still reach out to me after reading the article. I feel honored to help in any way I can.

I had one more medical event at the end of 2019, when the rest of my thyroid was removed. When the pathology came back favorably, it was a great relief. My hearing has never been as it was before the infection, but it has greatly improved over time. While 2020 and the following years would involve plenty of doctor's appointments, labs, and tests, I began to breathe easier again.

I will never be one of those people who say they are thankful for cancer. I fucking hate cancer. I'll never be the same. I'll never forget. The what-ifs are always there. Tests never get easier. Taking a pill every night is a daily dose of reality. But I used to feel like I couldn't go one second without thinking about cancer. Then gradually, I went an hour or two without it filling my mind, then a day or two, and now I go a week or more.

When I asked God for strength the night I got the diagnosis, I was really asking Him to take my cancer away. Instead, He gave me fortitude and a winding road that brought me to my knees more than once. But I am standing tall today, and you'd be hard-pressed to find many things besides grati- tude that can bring me to my knees now.

As 2019 wrapped up and I looked forward to

giving more time and energy to Girlilla Marketing again in the new year, I reflected not only on my experiences with cancer but also on how my illness impacted the business. I felt so grateful and lucky to have established a strong presence and industry reputation. While I had feared my illness might scare off some clients, many of them showed up wholeheartedly and sent us more work as a show of solidarity and support when we needed it most.

The music industry is a tight-knit world, a business of big dreams and taking big risks. The camaraderie among those of us who feel passionate about the industry is not only encouraging, it sustains all of us. We take care of one another. I learned that firsthand during my year of treatment. As the new year began, I couldn't wait to pay forward all the love and support I had received. Little did I know how many opportunities I'd have to do that in 2020.

CHAPTER TWENTY

The Whole World on Pause

· 2020 ·

AFTER MY RETURN to work in January 2020, I quickly fell back into my usual work-life routine. I'd stayed updated on everything work related, so there wasn't any catching up to do, per se. The biggest discovery was learning that the team could handle everything without me. This freed me from fighting to keep up on day-to-day details for every client and focus instead on managing the bigger picture and vision of the business.

My spirit was renewed by a new crop of younger, smart Girlillas, including Lindsey Feinstein, Conley Sweeney, and Alex Kinker. Millennials get a bad rap. These three ladies not only showed me what they were capable of professionally, they broke down a "boss barrier" I'd held up for a long time by showing me genuine compassion and concern that went far beyond an employer-employee dynamic.

I was looking forward to being more involved in charitable causes again. Just before my cancer diagnosis, Joe Galante, Sarah Trahern, and Tiffany Kerns had asked me to serve on the Country Music Association Foundation board. They refused to let me step down while I underwent treatment, did all the work for me, and invited me back for another round. Even though I couldn't be physically present as much as I wanted to be, I was able to read, ask questions, and understand the organization and their mission to provide music-education programs to more students.

Girlilla Marketing also began working in kind to support our friends at Music Health Alliance. We had offered advice here and there in the past, but now we dedicated resources to help expand Tatum Hauck Allsep's vision. Now that I was well again, I felt eager to contribute meaningfully to these wonderful causes.

* * *

In March 2020, like most businesses, we shut our office down in response to the COVID pandemic and went into the most extended period of remote work and crisis management we'd ever experienced. Only this time, it wasn't just a strategy for an isolated client or situation. It was the entire world.

As a business, we were already used to working from buses, planes, venues, and hotels. However, we always returned to home base and cherished our time to connect in person. The reality of not seeing clients and employees brought disbelief and, eventually, a little depression. While we at Girlilla Marketing weren't sure what this was going to mean for our clients or our business, all our training and expertise came into play.

There was a great need to stay connected and, with most of our clients, a great desire to help raise money, give people hope, entertain, and offer a break from struggles. The busy work of this scary season was a great distractor. We didn't have time to over-think our personal situations. Like everyone else, life seemed to be on shaky ground and, in some cases, in shambles. People around us were getting sick and losing their jobs and health insurance. Fear of the pandemic was at an all-time high, the political rhet-oric online was assaulting, and none of us had any idea when it would be over.

While our world was stressful, compared to our non-music-business friends and family members, we had community-based resources to lean on. We had associations willing to help us, banks ready to explain things to us, and each other to call.

It was our responsibility to keep the digital train on the tracks. As a type-A planner, I had to retrain myself to take what the day had to offer and do what I could. Things happened so fast and swung to such drastic extremes that flexibility was imperative.

Everyone had to adjust to the new rhythm of life. In the beginning months, it was rather exciting. Some weeks we'd have upwards of ten live streamed "concerts" or "live" events, and it was fun using Zoom. It was wonderful to see artists give free access to people purely to connect and entertain. They did this despite canceled tours, postponed productions, and having to make difficult decisions about laying people off, maxing out their credit cards to keep vendors like us on board, and worrying about their families and the world. It was nostalgic of the early days of social media when we didn't yet take the gift of being able to connect online for granted.

In the spring of 2020, we were still hopeful that our clients' tours would resume in the fall, movies and product lines would launch during the holiday season, and television production would be back in full swing after a few months. As things progressed in the wrong direction throughout the summer and fall and we understood that we'd be without live performances for most likely another year, our load grew heavier in terms of both work and personal duties.

Like everyone else, we felt pushed to our limit. We rallied, but frequently it was in shifts. Sometimes it was me ringing the bell, needing help because my husband was working too (somehow, he continued shooting a movie during this time). My kids were in and out of school frequently. Our former nanny, Holly, a new mom herself, brought her infant son, Burton, over and entertained the kids so I could continue working.

Luckily when one of us was down for the count, Ashley, Stevie, and I leaned on each other. We had a lot of touch-and-go moments as we figured things out, but we were a lean, loving, strong, focused team.

Clients who prospered through those shaky times shared a few things in common:

- They let go of the idea that everything needed to be a production.

- They realized that everyone was in the same boat, so they had some fun with the chaos and showed sides of themselves that were extremely endearing (even messing up when trying to figure out the technology).

- They were considerate of viewers' perceptions and contemplated the reception of posts from many different angles before posting.

- They realized that a lot of what we normally accomplished in person could be handled by phone/Zoom. (It was a good way to cut expenses.)

- Clients and team members alike had newfound respect for some of our work coming to a halt to take care of children or loved ones. For once, we weren't all trying to pretend that we were doing it all perfectly.

* * *

When I returned to work just before the pandemic shut everything down, I had felt so grateful to be back to my real life and able to focus on the business again. As the months of quarantine stretched on, fatigue set in. Analytics declined on the streams (fans had so many choices, and as with any good trend, the market grew oversaturated). People had watched all the on-demand content they could stomach. The internet—which rarely shocks me anymore— shocked with its depth of misinformation, negativity, and downright nastiness during the 2020 election.

After months of showing up as fully as possible for the business and our clients, as 2020 ended and COVID dragged on, for the first time in my career, I badly needed a break.

CHAPTER TWENTY-ONE

Social Media Reframe

· 2021 ·

THE TROUBLE WITH taking a break was that I felt guilty about doing so. I managed well throughout the quarantine. I kept the business going successfully and was able to pay my employees and keep us all on our health insurance. My husband and kids were doing fine. Yet a part of me felt like I'd been off work the previous year due to cancer. If I took any downtime during the pandemic, it would look bad. It wasn't rational, but I couldn't separate my role as CEO of Girlilla Marketing from my personal identity. I was burned out and feeling more and more like a martyr every day.

The push-pull between the part of me that insisted I needed a break and the part that resisted taking it made me irritable. I started spending more time online in my off hours, trying to distract myself from my self-inflicted frustration. I scrolled through post after post filled with images and cheery anecdotes about people who seemed to be living their best lives in quarantine—reading, working out, spending quality time with family, taking road trips, playing board games, and mastering gourmet charcuterie boards.

Rather than soothe my frustration, social media heightened it. When I compared my unkempt, chaotic, frazzled life to the carefully curated posts I read online, I felt like a failure. Why was I on so many Zoom meetings, yelling at my kids to be quiet, kicking my dogs out of my room, feeling annoyed at the sound of my husband breathing? Why was I eating all the crackers and taking showers only every couple of days? Suddenly I had FOMO (fear of missing out) and heavy-duty judgments about what people were posting and how they appeared to be living. I am not generally envious, so I tried to dissect my feelings. Why was I reacting so strongly? I was worn down from the last few years and much more susceptible to comparing myself unfavorably to others.

Something else about social media concerned me too. It was an election year in 2020, and political shenanigans were in full swing. Social causes were intertwined in those conversations and were unnecessarily and impolitely debated. The amount of misinformation and distortion posted by people I knew from all affiliations was incredibly disturbing. The many mean and aggressive comments that showed up in my feed baffled me. I found myself thinking frequently, *That can't possibly be my friend who believes that! That can't be a professional in my industry reposting that!*

Why were people spending their precious time reading, sharing, and commenting on things they should know might not be true? Why were good humans compelled to comment on others' profiles with condemnation and judgment? Why were we assuming that if an individual or a company didn't post about a social issue within a short amount of time (or ever) that it was a statement within itself?

Did anyone take the time to dissect the assault of information and thoughtfully decide how they wanted to take action? Was there room for differing opinions? Were people allowed to learn, grow, or change their minds anymore? Did shaming someone online ever shift their perspective?

I was deeply affected, and it exhausted me. People who express strong beliefs online can feel that other people aren't expressing themselves enough. People who want freedom to express themselves often don't want to extend that right to those with whom they disagree. Our freedom to be who we are, believe in what we believe, and let others do the same has been stripped away—by ourselves.

It's easy to blame the social networks. They make themselves easy targets with unscrupulous business practices. But the real problem is *us*. Suddenly, social media, a place of great innovation and connection (which has always had its dark side and problems, but the good outweighed the bad), felt more like a battlefield than a place to commune.

After the 2020 election and the holidays, I observed how I was feeling and reacting to social media. I had hoped, like many, that the political changeover and the new year would bring a much-needed fresh-start mentality. Thinking again of Pete's question and what else I still wanted to do in my life, I made a plan to strategically counter my fatigue and disenchantment. As much as I could in my line of work, I curbed my online scrolling. I muted or blocked a lot of people who I love. I unfollowed profiles that I previously relied on for news if they were inciting sensationalistic and antagonistic views.

I took a big breath whenever friends fought with one another or argued with strangers online. I imagined all these people together at a dinner party, discussing the world's events, and I visualized everyone listening more, talking less. I tried to imagine what kind of middle ground we could meet in if we remembered that most of us are doing the best we can.

Idealistic? Perhaps.

Crazy? I don't think so.

I thought about the hundreds of conversations I'd had about not only marketing but the broader spectrum of social and digital communication. Marketers, artists, brands, advertisers, parents... everyone was tired, bewildered, unsure of the future, yet not willing to make big changes. We've watched the movies, read the articles, detoxed from social media, and yet we've ended up with more profiles, more worries, and more anxiety. Why?

For over ten years, I'd moved with the times because it was my job. But now I was feeling something else. It was the same sense of mission and purpose I'd felt when Pete asked me what I'd do if I knew my life was half over.

Just as I wanted to advocate for early detection after my mammogram caught my cancer, I wanted to guide changes in social media based on my industry expertise and my heartfelt passion for helping humanity. I felt a responsibility to change the environment. If that wasn't feasible, I wanted to help alter how people feel about and react to social media.

The impacts of social media had been sitting heavy in my gut for years. For all that time, I didn't feel I could change it. I hoped maybe someone smarter than I—more technical, more influential— would do it. But now I see that it must be all of us. I couldn't in good conscience blindly chase algorithms for fans and followers, knowing it was affecting lives (including my own). The media isn't going to stop assaulting us. The platforms aren't going to do the right things. It's up to us, together.

I want to be known for who I am, not for what I post (or don't). I don't want to judge or be judged. I want to help and be helped. I want to double down on what's good and change what needs changing.

We have the greatest power: the click, the share, the comment. When we stop, it stops.

I've been uniquely engaged with social media from its earliest days. In the beginning, we all looked at real life and determined what would be good to capture and share publicly on the outlets. Now, we deliberately create and stage "moments" for our social personas, in hopes of gaining more clicks and engagement. This posturing dramatically impacts our lives. I mentioned earlier that social media used to excite me for its potential to create community. But we've all seen firsthand how it can also distort, alienate, and fracture our connections with one another. This scares me more than anything.

We hunt and pick on each other online. Sure, these platforms and their algorithms love turmoil (engagement), but you are responsible for your own behavior and reaction to the bait. I predict we will all be mortified looking back at the last couple of years and how much we hid behind social media in lieu of real human interaction. We will be embarrassed about the articles we shared without reading and verifying first. We will regret the hours we spent arguing with strangers or commenting to incite reaction when we knew it wouldn't result in any real advancement. I am confident that we will regret how we treated people online. I'm sure we will ask ourselves how we blamed our comments, clicks, and shares on anyone but ourselves. It is not acceptable to spread rumors and gossip, but we did it.

We have the power to control our online experiences. Let's not give it away. Who you are online is an extension of who you are in real life. Carefully consider what you feel compelled to comment on or share before blindly clicking or reacting and regretting it later. By exercising restraint, you leave openings for important issues to have the stage. If you are having a hard time with your reaction toward certain outlets or people, block them, unfollow, or use your mute button. These tools are there for a reason! Not everything deserves your energy.

If you are a creator, create more and worry

less. Consistently produce compelling content and interact with people on a level that you can keep up with. Ask yourself before posting: *Is this post going to create value for my audience? Will this post engage and perhaps increase my audience?* If your post doesn't fit in either of these buckets, reconsider posting it. Keep the focus on what is making you happy to create, and the rest will follow in time.

Everything we need to know about how to act and interact online we learned in preschool. Here's a top-ten cheat sheet, should you need a reminder:

1. Be nice.

2. Say you're sorry when you make a mistake.

3. Take turns.

4. Say please and thank you.

5. Listen before talking (or posting).

6. Give praise.

7. Use your manners.

8. Be patient.

9. Respect personal space.

10. Don't play with your weiner in public.

There's nothing like a life-threatening illness to make you contemplate what will remain as your legacy after you die. I've already lived out my answers to Pete's question about what I would do if I knew my life was half over. And I've come up with more goals to achieve.

It still boggles my mind that a girl with a dream can pack up her Jeep and pursue her aspirations armed with only passion, grit, and determination. When I think of how many hands lifted me up along the way and how many wonderful people continue to give me support, I cannot do anything other than be grateful and pay it forward.

If you have loyal, long-term employees, you are successful. If you have loyal, long-term employees who turn out to be friends, you are downright rich. I played soccer as a kid and really enjoyed being on a team. The camaraderie at Girlilla Marketing continues to remind me daily how fun it is to create and win with others. I am grateful for Girlilla Marketing's employees every day. There has been nothing more fulfilling professionally than collaborating with my staff. I can't imagine anything more rewarding than working with people I trust with my professional and personal life. All of us accept one another unconditionally, and we work together to get the best possible results for our clients.

* * *

As of the writing of this book in 2024, Girlilla Marketing has celebrated over fifteen years in the business. My hope and intention are that in the years ahead the company continues to flourish and thrive by serving our clients wholeheartedly to the best of our collective abilities.

Moving forward, I plan to take a more active role in advocating for healthy social media use, including setting boundaries and limits on usage and content. Can social media be a wonderful tool for connection? Absolutely. But it must not be the only place we go to for validation or to feel understood.

Social media must not be the place from which we source our self-worth. It must not be the only place from which we seek information or communicate.

Making small changes in how we interact online and advocating for better barriers to data and stronger controls for privacy is my wish for all of us in the social media arena. Keeping our common sense and humanity intact when we are logged on is a simple blueprint to safety and success.

I am extremely hopeful for the future. Being connected is a beautiful thing. I'm so grateful that I—and Girlilla Marketing—get to participate and contribute to humanity's evolution at this remarkable intersection of artistic creativity and technological innovation.

I Couldn't Have Done It Without You

To THE BEST DECISION I've ever made, thank you, **Shannon Houchins**, for being my partner in all things life and love. You are my superhero. To my favorite humans on the planet, **Daphne** and **Chess**, thank you for choosing me to be your mom and allowing me the privilege of watching you grow; it's the greatest joy of my life. To my sister, **Kelley**—it's always been you and me when it counted. You were mean as hell as a big sister, and I am grateful for every second of it. To my beautiful niece, **Ava**, I love you, Toots. To my brother-in-law, **Jeff**, you are the brother I never wanted, but after all these years, I guess you're okay. To my stepdaughters, **Cassidy** and **Lunden**, I am in your corner. To all my fur babies, present and who've crossed the rainbow bridge, Mama loves you. Special shout-out to **Lola** and **Claud Von Dog**, both of whom, I believe, were my soul dogs and were sent straight from heaven to love me.

To the family I chose: **Shelby Shirk**, **Candice Towey**, and **Robyn Haun**. Sorry about the '90s… and let's be honest, part of the 2000s. Love you gals so much and can't imagine doing life without you. To **Holly Harrell**, you are a blessing to our family. **Linde Thurman** and **Ana Vincent**, I hit the lottery being in your orbit; thank you for loving and taking care of me as the mom/friends I needed. To my circle of friends—you know who you are, and I hope I've learned enough to tell you often how loved you are.

To **Girlilla Marketing**, the house that built me. There's nothing more gratifying than coming into the office every day and being happy to do so. To my other life partners, **Ashley Alexander** and **Stevie Escoto**, you are truly the best and without you, I'd make really bad decisions (fun... but bad). To **Lindsey Feinstein**, **Conley Sweeney**, and **Alex Kinker**, you came along at a time when I wasn't sure I wanted to keep growing and you inspired me to do so. Present Girlilla team, **Maddie Cannatella**, **Catherine Bagwell**, **Haley Hansen**, and **Taylor Rupp**... the best we've ever had. Special thanks to **Gigi Morrison** for pushing us forward creatively. Now, get back to work! Past Girlilla employees, the good and bad experiences made me better in equal parts. I have gratitude for all these lessons.

To my professional village, **Michelle Beeler** and **Mike Vaden**, who treated me like a million bucks when I had nothing. Mike, you are the best damn business manager I know. Michelle, you are so important to me. **Scott Safford** and **Jonathan Motley**, first day on the job came with a subpoena—can't beat those legal odds! **Will Jackson** and **Cahaba Wealth Management**, thanks for making me plan like an adult and ensure my team does as well. To **Jennifer Alexander**, **Amy Dodgen**, and the Pinnacle team, your partnership is so much more than banking. To **Tatum Hauck Allsep**, **Sarah Trahern**, **Joe Galante**, and **Tiffany Kerns**—I know you're on a whole lot of confidant and mentor lists, but you will always be at the top of mine.

Luckily through marriage (and divorce), I've been connected to an extended family who I am grateful for, including two beautiful stepdaughters, grand-parents, grandchildren, aunts, uncles, and cousins. While it's confusing who is related to who, all these humans make up a village I am proud to be a part of. Thank you to **the Lombardos, the Houchins, Nina, the Kisslers, the Statens, the Cromies,** and **the Balls.**

To my survivor circle, I am eternally grateful for your humor and grace during the worst party to ever be invited to. Thank you for keeping me sane and uplifted and being an example of how to help others. To my medical circle—when it was dicey, I clung onto **Dr. Katie M Davis**, **Dr. Kent Higdon**, **Dr. John W. Seibert** (plus **Nurse Susan!**), **Dr. Celeste Hemingway**, **Dr. Catherine Linn**, **Dr. Kaylin S. Craig**, **Tiffani Werthan**, and so many more at Vanderbilt Medical Center. Thank you.

I am so grateful to our clients and partners. A business like mine can't make it this many years without free flowing loyalty and trust mixed with a healthy dose of humor. I get to learn as much as I teach.

To my editor and now my friend, **Bridget Boland**, thank you, and thank the Universe for plopping you into my life at the right time. Your guidance, patience, and partnership are valued wholeheartedly. You're the quickest reader on the planet, and even though in my head I said, *WTF?* when you made me close my eyes to listen to my own writing, you were right. You're always right.

Big thanks to my friends and colleagues who walked down memory lane with me (and proofread it). I did my best to keep my memories honest. **Rebekah Gordon**, you read the worst version; hope this one is better. **Cindy Hunt**, you have the kindest, gentlest red pen on the planet. I am so grateful for you and **Heather Conley**. **Sarah Skates**, when I get "good" from you, I feel validated. **Jay DeMarcus**, your encouragement was paramount. Extra high fives for the beautiful humans who took time to read and endorse this book.

Becky Nesbitt, from the first conversation we had, I knew you were my person. Your faith in me and strength of the team at **Forefront Books** and **Resolve Editions** has been an amazing experience for me. Thank you to **Jill Smith**, **Jennifer Gingerich**,

Acknowledgments

Lauren Ward, **Landry Parkey**, **Natalie Lowe**, **Mary Sue Oleson**, and **Kate Etue** for your help in bringing this dream alive!

I have been inspired, molded, loved, and pushed by a massive community of people who could take up a whole book. I am sure I forgot to call and thank someone important to me because I still have holes in my brain from all that E in the '90s, but I tried my best on GirlillaMarketing.com.

To anyone I ever worked for as an employee or whoever dated me—sorry about all that.

Be good… online and in real life,

Jennie

About the Author

JENNIE SMYTHE is Founder and Chief Executive Officer of award-winning Girlilla Marketing, which heads digital strategy for a diverse roster of world-famous entertainers and brands, including Dead & Company, Willie Nelson, Darius Rucker, Blondie, Brooke Shields, Iliza Shlesinger, Terry Crews, Kristin Chenoweth, Vince Gill, and many others. Smythe is a forward-thinking entrepreneur who leads runs her self-built company with equal parts passion and drive.

Girlilla Marketing celebrated fifteen years of success in 2023. The talented team oversees social media endeavors, partner marketing, and content creation for clients. They bring expert knowledge to developing online audiences, digital monetization, virtual events, fan clubs, paid media campaigns, analytics tracking, and creative services, such as graphic design and video editing.

In her more than two decades of experience, it is no accident that Smythe has emerged on top of this ever-evolving field. Motivated by a lifelong love of music, her creative approach has earned numerous awards and recognition. She has been featured in *Forbes*, the *Associated Press*, *Billboard*, *MusicRow*, *Fast Company*, *People*, *HITS*, and *The Tennessean*. She is a multi-year winner of the *Nashville Business Journal*'s Women in Music City Awards, a *MusicRow* magazine Rising Women on the Row honoree, and was included on the *Nashville Post* "In Charge 2023: Music" list.

Becoming Girlilla is an honest and witty journey through her formative years, career growth, breast cancer diagnosis, the pandemic, and the lessons learned along the way. "I hope that I can make you think, laugh, and see your own story in mine," she says, "because we are all connected, online and offline."

Smythe is chairperson of the Country Music Association and board of directors and is on the boards of the CMA Foundation (past chairperson) and Music Health Alliance. She is a past board member of the Academy of Country Music and a graduate of the prestigious Leadership Music executive development program. Her early career includes time at Disney's Hollywood Records, YAHOO! Music, Warner Bros. Records, and Clear Channel.

Smythe is married to fellow entrepreneur, Shannon Houchins, and resides in Nashville with their two children.

To learn more, please visit
www.GirlillaMarketing.com.